The Ultimate Solution of the American Negro Problem

EDWARD EGGLESTON

ISBN: 978-1-63923-774-6

Printed: March 2023

Published and Distributed By:
Lushena Books
607 Country Club Drive, Unit E
Bensenville, IL 60106
www.lushenabks.com

ISBN: 978-1-63923-774-6

CONTENTS

CONTENTS

PREFACE

In the early chapters of this volume I have attempted to place this important economic and social problem on a strictly scientific footing. And when I use the word "science," I mean ascertained facts, accumulated, systematized knowledge, formulated for the discovery of general laws. Whether or not I have succeeded in this remains to be determined by the impartial reader. If my scientific bases prove to have been well founded I believe it will be admitted that the work presents the key to the situation. No doubt it will appear to some that I have gone too much into detail and presented facts, figures and illustrations that do not directly bear upon the theme. In other words the foundation may seem too heavy for the superstructure. To this I reply: that if by such elaboration the scientific matter contained in the first six chapters has been established in the mind of the reader as the true origin, descent and quality of the Negro mind and character I have succeeded in the task set before me. The rest of the book is largely dependent upon the admission of the fundamental truths set forth in these early chapters. Regarding the accuracy of my deductions and predictions, the intelligent reader and future history constitute the just and logical arbitors.

It remains to be added that statistics of the thirteenth census—just now available—completely confirm my predictions concerning the relative numerical decline of the Negro during the decade ending with 1910. None of these figures were available until after my manuscript was ready for the press.

For many courtesies and valuable aid in securing

information I am greatly indebted to the Virginia State Library and through it to the Congressional Library at Washington. Likewise I acknowledge indebtedness to many studious friends who have aided with suggestions and reviews of my manuscripts.

Darwin, Amelia, Va., Sept. 1, 1912.

The Ultimate Solution of The American Negro Problem

CHAPTER I

The Birth and Early History of Man

IN writing on "The Negro Problem" we cannot consistently omit either the birth or the early history of the race; and in view of the fact that we all came primarily from a common stock it becomes necessary to inquire briefly into its natural descent, and try to fathom the mysteries which once shrouded the birth of our earliest ancestors.

In most writings on the race question the subject has been taken up piecemeal, as it were, disjointedly and unscientifically. The writer sometimes selecting as his starting point the importation of Negro slaves into the American colonies, and again he begins with Lincoln's Emancipation Proclamation, and so on. No such writing, however cleverly done, can hope to lucidate this question; nor can it present to the mind of the reader a complete picture of the Negro character.

In considering the ultimate solution of the problem—and what can, or what should be done with, or for, our Negro population—the mind must be supplied with the facts of causation, which latter have produced both the race and its present environment. We must know why, and wherein it differs from the white race in order to consider intelligently possible remedies for our present problem.

The importation of Negroes into the American colonies seemed to commend itself as a suitable starting point when this work was first contemplated;

7

but very little reflection was needed to convince us of the necessity of introducing these early chapters, setting forth the conditions under which the human race came into existence, and how it came to be divided into the several, more or less distinct, varieties.

In the absence of the information contained in this, and the three or four immediately succeeding chapters, it is quite impossible for the student to possess any adequate conception of the subject in hand. There are many reasons—which will be seen later on—why we cannot understand the real deficiencies of the Negro, or the menace of his presence to the white population, without some elementary knowledge of the influence of environment and of inherited traits and tendencies. Therefore we have undertaken to supply the essential truths of the birth and early history of Man.

From the overthrow of the Western Roman Empire by the barbarians in the latter part of the fifth century (476 B. C.) to the taking of Constantinople, or the discovery of America, in the fifteenth century, constitutes one of the most remarkable periods in history. This era is generally referred to as the Middle Ages, or Dark Ages. Superstition was rife and the unusual or extraordinary in nature always implied a miracle as its only possible explanation. Since that time, however, Man's powers of investigation and of exposing the truths of nature's mysteries have increased with marvelous rapidity. Thus in very recent years Man has intruded upon the secret storehouses of nature, and among many other discoveries he has brought forth her anthropoid models, from which Man himself was made. Now it is important to define the starting point of the race as clearly as possible, and in doing this it is well to recognize the serious difficulties which we are to meet.

Unfortunately, we think—but true nevertheless—the people of our own country, as elsewhere, are strongly inclined to hold fast to arbitrary and unreasoned opinions upon such subjects. A still more regrettable circumstance is the tendency on the part of the so-called well-educated and influential minority to accept without investigation, or due consideration, doctrines propagated by interested partisans and self-constituted teachers, who for the most part are actuated by ulterior motives. This apparent lack of independent reflection is strikingly singular when we consider the further fact that our country is *theoretically* a land of free citizens, civilized and cultivated to a degree never before known in the history of the world.

In a court of justice the law requires that all available evidence be presented and carefully weighed before an opinion is formulated; and just so it should be when we come to consider this mooted "American Negro Problem." We should hold no preconceived views as relics of the War Between the States, nor as heirlooms of our ancestors; but as intelligent men and women it behooves us to demand the evidence, both for and against our black brother, before judgment is passed upon him.

On account of this attitude of unwillingness to be convinced, and determination not to alter or modify fixed opinions, we cannot consider the scientific account of the natural development of the human race without arousing some opposition—a regrettable but unavoidable circumstance.

To begin with then, that beautiful scriptural allegory, contained in the first, second, and third chapters of the book of Genesis (King James' English

Translation), of Adam and Eve in the Garden of Eden, will always hold its high place in the world's literature; but no one, apart from the illiterate and the unreasoning, now regards it seriously in connection with the birth and early history of the race. Consequently we take up our subject with the birth of Man as revealed to us by modern scientific research.

Man, then, is unquestionably the product of natural forces operating through many millions of years. The matter that now constitutes the earth once existed as an attenuated gas with a temperature so high that life would have been impossible even if conditions could have been in other respects suitable. It had first to cool down and solidify, and then certain portions of its surface had to fall below a temperature of 212 degrees Fahrenheit (boiling point), before the spontaneous generation of life in any form was possible. This it finally did, and sometime subsequent to this geological period—we know not when—and under conditions totally different from anything within our limited experience, a low form of life came into existence.

The chemical constitution of certain particles of matter was changed from that condition known as inorganic (non-vital), to that defined as organic (vital). It was, of course, the very lowest form of life. The sponge and the oyster—two familiar forms of animal life—are, comparatively speaking, high in the scale of living things. It was a mere cell life, protoplasmic matter, in which it would have been barely possible for the modern physiologist to detect its vital nature.

Ever since this marvelous happening natural forces have been constantly at work, transforming the lower into the higher orders of living things, until, in the fullness of time, primitive Man was evolved.   In our judgment, this historic fact ranks all others, as the most significant event since the beginning of the world.   Hear the great physiologist, the illustrious Huxley, in this connection:

"The question of questions for mankind—the problem which underlies all others, and is more deeply interesting than any other—is the ascertainment of the place which Man occupies in nature and his relation to the universe of things.   Whence our race has come; what are the limits of our power over nature, and of nature's power over us; to what goal are we tending; are the problems which present themselves anew and with undiminished interest to every man born into the world."

No doubt, for thousands of generations our ancestors were in an intermediary state of transformation, during which they could not have been definitely classed as either Man or beast.   However, there are certain ascertained facts regarding the birth of the race, which have been worked out with a great deal of accuracy by recent investigators.   For instance, all the evidence points to a common ancestry.   Every creature that has reached that rung in the ladder of evolutionary progress upward, entitling him to be classed as Man, is believed to have come originally from a single pair.

Geology and Anthropology (the study of the structure of the earth and the study of the human kind, respectively) are the principal branches of science concerned in the past history of the world and of prehistoric Man.   Modern geologists and other scientists have amply demonstrated that the world itself is the product of orderly change, from simplicity to complexity (from relative homogeneity to relative heterogeneity), under the universal law of evolution,

and that Man also is a product of this law. Therefore we hold, in common with the rest of the scientific world, that it is established truth that Man's
place in nature is that of the highest representative
of the animal kingdom. This fact being established
we will now turn our attention more directly to the
birth and early environment of Man, and try to pen-
etrate the veil of the ages which has, until very recently, shrouded the subject in an inscrutable darkness
from time immemorial.

THE MISSING LINK

By very recent and exhaustive investigations it has
been definitely determined that the Eastern Archipelago is the birthplace of the race; and that evidence
brought to light in 1894, by Dr. Eugene Dubois,
makes it almost as certain that the still more definite
cradle of our first ancestors is the island of Java. In
what is known as the Trinil district of this island
there are certain rock-beds which belong to a geological period of more than passing interest, called the
late Tertiary period. In order to more accurately
define an age so rich in fossil remains, the late Sir
Charles Lyell assigned to it the name "Pliocene." It
was in the island of Java, in these rock-beds of the
Trinil district, in the year 1894, that Dr. Dubois discovered the most extraordinary and significant fossil
remains that *terra firma* has yet vouchsafed to arch-
aelogy. Much animated, and at times acrimonious,
debate was caused by this discovery; and since the
turmoil and smoke of battle have been wafted hence
on the wings of time, sober scientific opinion has declared these petrified remains to have belonged to one
of the earliest, indeed one of the very first members
of the human race. These human bones had long
been sought for; Darwin and other naturalists of his

time knew, and affirmed, that such primitive specimens of the race once existed; and geologists held
that it was more than probable that somewhere in
the *Pliocene* rocks their bones must have been preserved, if modern Man could only have the good for-
tune to come upon them.

The importance then of this discovery, and the
assertion that it connects the human race with lower
animals, justify some mention of the evidence which
supports it; otherwise, those who are naturally skep-
tical might be inclined to relegate these statements
to the sphere of pure fiction.

To this remarkable find Dr. Dubois himself gave
the name, *"Pithecanthropus Erectus,"* which is, being
interpreted, an ape-man that could walk. These fossil remains consist of a skullcap,—the upper half of
the skull, including the orbits of the eyes—a femur
(thigh-bone), and two teeth. As we have said, the
discovery was made in 1894. The location from
which these bones were taken is the left bank of the
river Bengawan, Java. The nature of the geological formation, from which these invaluable remains
were secured, is described as a conglomerate, which
lies upon a bed of marine marl and sand of *Pliocene*
age.

For years after this concrete acquisition to our store
of knowledge of human development an animated debate went on among scientists of all lands, as to the
exact value and proper classification of this ape-like
man, or man-like ape, as the case might be. Finally,
in 1896—some two years subsequent to Dubois's discovery—those fossil remains were put on trial at the
third International Zoological Congress, held at Leyden, one of the oldest and most famous cities of the
Netherlands. The result of this Leyden court of
inquiry was, that out of twelve recognized experts

present, three held that the bones belonged to a very low order of Man; three declared that they were the remains of a man-like ape, of extraordinary stature; while the remaining six affirmed that they belonged to an intermediary form, which directly connected primitive Man with certain extinct anthropoid apes.

Could the evidence of a discovered "missing link" be clearer? It is vouched for by Dr. A. H. Keane, the distinguished author, and student of anthropology. In his work entitled "The World's Peoples" Dr. Keane says:

"Here also the line of human ascent, as traced through the Javanese 'missing link,' is seen to spring, not from any of these higher anthropoids (man-like ape), as is popularly supposed, but from a common simian (ape) stem having its roots far back in the Miocene (Middle Tertiary) epoch. In this 'first Man,' as he is designated, the erect position, as shown by the perfectly human thigh-bone, implies a perfectly prehensile (grasping) hand, with opposable thumb, the chief instrument of human progress, while the cranial capacity suggests vocal organs sufficiently developed for the first rude utterance of articulate speech."

The great German biologist and popular scientific writer, Dr. Ernst Haeckel, not only accepted the find of Dubois as positive proof of the simian origin of the human race but forthwith published a book on the subject, entitled, "The Last Link," in which he offers the most incontrovertible evidence, from the standpoint of a great expert; that these remains present to us the physical proofs of what science had long since declared to be true; that Man came to his position of transcendent superiority over his fellow-creatures by a slow metamorphosis (transformation) from lower forms. It seems to be proven truth then, that Man is the product of natural forces, operating through millions of years. But as we have said the average human mind is singularly reluctant to change its long established conceptions of truth, and especially is this true when their view-point is the result of youthful training and transmitted ancestral tendencies—as is the case in this instance—even when confronted with the most positive and conclusive evidence. Therefore it is important to impress upon the reader the truths of geology concerning the slowness of these transformatory processes.

THE SLOWNESS OF METAMORPHOSIS

Naturally enough does the man who has not given his time and thought to the study of nature say, "I see no evidence of change and the transformation of species about me; why should I conclude that such has ever taken place?" And an orderly sequence of ideas suggests the further question: How much time has nature required to effect these changes? To the latter query we answer: Perhaps not less than fifty million years have passed away since life first appeared on the earth. And millions of years intervened; indeed we might almost say æons of time elapsed after the first spontaneous generation of life, before Man was evolved.

Geologists and anthropologists believe the total existence of the human race to have covered a period of twenty million years or more. Thus it is highly probable that the computation mentioned above, in connection with the earliest appearance of life in any form, is inadequate, and that twice that time would more nearly express the truth. However this may be, it is very certain that when we begin to deal with such enormous lapses of time, ordinary figures and methods of expression convey little or no mental impression. Therefore we shall endeavor to present the matter in another form.

In order to obviate this objection astronomers use "light-years"—that is the space traversed by a ray of light in a twelve months—for their unit of time; but perhaps another form of expression will serve our purpose still better:

Picture in your mind if you can the time that has intervened between the birth of Christ and the present moment—a period that has witnessed the birth, history, and death of some sixty generations. Now let us adopt this era as our unit, and substitute it for year. Man, then, to attain his present estate—and since he diverged from the parent stem—has required ten thousand, four hundred Christian eras, when reckoned by the lowest scientific estimate. (Many authorities would multiply this computation by five). In our own opinion, and in all human probability, Man, as such, has been roaming the earth, in his present upright posture and possessed of some rude form of articulate speech, for at least twenty thousand Christian eras. Nearly every scientific chronological revision places both the first appearance of life and the birth of Man, at a more remote date. These fundamental truths of geology and anthropology, regarding the almost inconceivable æons of time requisite for natural law to develop Man, with his transcendent intellect, are of prime importance, since such performances are incomprehensible under any other hypothesis.

In former times there apparently existed a great divide or gulf between Man and his brute ancestors, which placed in the hands of the principal enemy of science a mighty weapon which it wielded fiercely and furiously from pulpit and press; but the well-authenticated and abundant evidence of the discovery of the "link," which spans the famous chasm, seems to have paralyzed the strong right arm of dogmatic theology and those who would deny the development of the human kind from lower forms. As a result of this victory, science, with the consciousness of a battle won, is enjoying the proverbial and peaceful calm which follows the mighty storm.

The dominant characteristic of humanity is vanity: "Vanity of vanities, sayeth the preacher; all is vanity." This inordinate egotism even more than religious tradition and superstition, seems to have repelled the masses from the acceptance of the truth. The scientist sees no humiliation or disgrace about the discovery of Man's simian origin, but in the eyes of the masses its only redeeming virtue is the assurance that he is verily the lord and master of creation, preeminently superior to every other living thing.

MAN'S EARLY PROGRESS AND MENTAL DEVELOPMENT

Having discovered the facts concerning Man's origin, as well as the geographical location of his birth, let us pry into the secret chests that contain the hidden treasures of his early progress and mental development.

In view of our animal ancestry we are forced to conclude that many faculties, formerly computed as strictly human, necessarily had their beginning in pre-human brutes. The cranial capacity of the highest living apes is something like five hundred cubic centimetres; whereas the Javanese link had a capacity of about one thousand cubic centimetres, which latter is approximately half way between the highest present-day ape and the Caucasian, or European white man; thus showing the brute ancestors of our first human parents to have been creatures of no mean intellectual powers, and that Man, in the outset, inherited a very respectable cranial capacity.*

Dr. Ernst Haeckel, in his work entitled "The History of Creation," in the chapter on "Development of Man," says:

"Those processes of development which led to the origin of the most Man-like apes must be looked for in the two adaptational changes which, above all others, contributed to the making of Man, namely, upright walk and articulate speech. These two physiological functions necessarily originated together with two morphological transmutations, with which they stand in the closest correlation, namely, the differentiation of the two pairs of limbs and the differentiation of the larynx. The important perfecting of these organs and their functions must have necessarily and powerfully reacted upon the differentiation of the brain and the mental activities dependent upon it, and thus have paved the way for the endless career in which Man has since progressively developed, and in which he has far outstripped his animal ancestors."

In his book entitled "The World's Peoples," the famous anthropologist and author, Dr. A. H. Keane, refers in the most confident way to the Javanese "missing link" and speaks of it as if the entire world recognized it to be a creature intermediary between man and the lower animals, in an actual state of metamorphosis.

Clearly then this Javanese man was already fairly well equipped for his long and perilous journeyings

---

*This standard of cranial capacity, as an index to intellectual powers, is by no means accurate, and cannot be used as a criterion among individuals; but as a broad general index for comparing fossil remains, lower animals, and present-day human beings, it serves fairly well. Moreover, at least so far as concerns fossil remains, it is practically the only test of relative intellectual capacity at our command.

round the globe. His weapons of offense and defense consisted chiefly of stones, wooden clubs, and
the large thigh-bones of his own kind. Gifted, as he
was, with mental powers far beyond all other animals,
his future success and continued progress were assured.

Since all the facts we can command would lead to the
belief that this "first man," as he is sometimes called,
had no knowledge of navigation the question naturally
arises, how did he, or his progeny, escape from the
island birthplace of the race? Geologists assure us
that he was not confronted with this barrier; that
the physical geography of the period was totally different from the present divisions of land and water;
and that there were land connections from the present
island of Java to both Asia and Africa. The road
was open across the Indian Ocean to Madagascar
and South Africa by the Indo-African Continent, now
long since submerged. The Eastern Archipelago,
which included the island of Java, at that time still
formed part of the Asiatic mainland, from which it
is even now only slightly separated by shallow waters,
in many places less than fifty fathoms deep. East-
ward the road was open to New Guinea and across
Terres Strait to Australia, thence through the Louis-
ade Islands to the Pacific Ocean, which is now known
to be a region of subsidence. Thus Dr. Klaatsch,
who in 1904 studied the question on the spot, concludes that the peopling of Australia can be explained
only by a former land connection, with a central point
of distribution (such as Java) from which in one direction has been distributed the Asiatic races, and in
another the Australian aborigines. In the northern
hemisphere Europe could be reached by three different routes; one across the Strait of Gibraltar; another between Tunis, Malta, Sicily, and Italy; and a

third from Cyrenacia across the Agean to Greece, and thence from the mainland of Europe to the British Isles via the Strait of Dover and the shallow North Sea. Lastly the New World was accessible from Asia across Bering Strait, and from Europe through the Orkneys, the Shetlands, the Faroes, Iceland, and Greenland. Here were, therefore, sufficient land connections for primitive Man to have spread from his Javanese cradle to the uttermost parts of the earth. That he did so spread in very early (Pleistocene or even Pliocene) times is well established, as will presently be shown. While the routes here suggested may seem speculative to some, it is highly probable that they are correct, since we have the best of evidence that these and no others existed during the Middle or late *Tertiary* period.

"Much trustworthy evidence has been collected to show that the whole world had really been peopled during this period," says Keane, "which roughly coincides with the Ice Age, when a large part of the northern and southern hemispheres was subject to recurrent invasions of thick-ribbed ice advancing successively from both poles. The migrations were most probably begun in pre-glacial times—that is, before the appearance of the first great ice-wave, then arrested and resumed alternately with the long interglacial intervals, thus advancing and receding with the spread and retreat of the ice-cap, and completed in the post-glacial or early *Pleistocene* epoch say some two or three hundred thousand years ago. At that time the various wandering groups had already made considerable progress both in physical and mental respects, as is seen in the Neanderthal skull, which is the oldest yet found in Europe, standing midway between the Javanese ape-man and the present low races. All were still very much alike, presenting a sort of generalized human type which may be called Pleistocene man, a common undeveloped form, which did not begin to specialize—that is to evolve the existing varieties—until the several *Pleistocene* groups reached their present zoological domains. We know from the study of extinct and existing animal forms how, for instance, the Camel family, which probably originated in North America, is now represented by such allied species as the guanaco, vicuna and llama in South America, and the baktrian and Arabian camel in Asia. It was the same with the human family, which, originating in Malaysia, is now represented all over the world by four main varieties with their endless sub-varieties; Negroes or Blacks in the Sudan, South Africa, and Oceania (Australia); Mongol or Yellow in Central, North and East Asia; Amerinds (Red or Brown) in the New World; and Caucasians (white and also Dark) in North Africa, Europe, Irania, India, western Asia aad Polynesia.

"The four main divisions of mankind are thus seen to have been evolved independently in their several zones from Pleistocene ancestral groups of somewhat uniform physical type and all sprung from a common Pliocene prototype. This view of human origins at once removes the greatest difficulty hitherto presented by the existing varieties, which, being sprung separately in separate areas from a common parent stem, need no longer be derived one from another—white from black, yellow from red, and so on—a crude notion which both on physiological and geographic grounds has always remained an inscrutable puzzle to serious students of mankind. To suppose that some highly specialized group, say, originally black, migrating from continent to continent, became white in one region and yellow in another, is a violent assumption which could never be verified and is opposed to the natural relations. Such a group passing from its proper zone to another essentially different environment must inevitably have died out long before it had time to become acclimatized. The fundamental racial characters are the result of slow adaptation to their special surroundings. They are what climate, soil, diet, heredity, natural selection, and time have made them, and are of too long standing to be effaced or blurred except by miscegenation, a process which assumes the existence of other specialized forms, and as above seen is rendered possible by primordial unity.

"By common descent and separate local development is further explained the surprising resemblance which is everywhere presented both by the earliest remains and the earliest works of primitive Man. Such are the fossil or semi-fossil skulls found in Europe, Egypt, Mongolia, and the New World, and the stone instruments occurring in vast quantities in Britain, France, Belgium, North and South Africa, India, North and South America from British Columbia to Terra del Fuego. Certain Australian skulls seem cast in the same mould as the above mentioned Neanderthal, while rude stone instruments brought from the most distant lands are so alike in form and character that they might have been made by the same hands. On the Banks of the Nile objects of European type have been discovered, and others collected in Somaliland might have been dug out of the drift deposits of the Seine, the Thames or the ancient Solent (Sir John Evans). The Pleistocene or Quarternary epoch, as represented by those objects of primitive culture, ranged over a vast period of time which has been conveniently divided into two great epochs, the Palæolithic or Old Stone, and the Neolithic or New Stone Age, these being so named from the material chiefly used by primitive peoples in the manufacture of their weapons and other implements. The distinction between the two periods, which are not to be taken as time sequences since they overlap in many places, is based essentially on the different treatment of the material, which during the immeasurably longer Old Stone Age was at first merely chipped, flaked, or otherwise rudely fashioned, but in the New more carefully worked and polished. Evidence is, however, now accumulating to show that progress was continuous throughout the whole of the first cultural era, which thus tended in favorable localities such as South France, the Riviera, and North Africa to merge imperceptibly in the second, so that it is not always possible to draw any clear line between the Old and the New Stone Age. In one respect the former was towards its close even in advance of the latter, and quite a 'Pralaeolithic School of Art' was developed during a long inter—or post-glacial period of steady progress in the sheltered Vizere valley of Dordogne, South France. Here were produced some of those remarkable stone, horn and even ivory scrapers, gravers, harpoons, ornaments and statuettes with carvings on the round, and skilful etchings of seals, fishes, reindeer, harnessed horses, mammoths, snakes, and man himself, which also occur in other districts."*

---

*There is much archæological evidence of the Old and New Stone Ages and of the abodes and occupations of a race that dwelt upon the earth during both these periods—which together cover not less than three hundred thousand years—but its introduction is not essential to our purposes and, while intensely interesting and instructive to some, might prove tiresome to others. For these reasons much of the record of prehistoric Man is omitted.

After these two Stone Ages came the Metal Ages which, while covering many thousands of years, were of shorter duration than the Stone Ages. Later still came what we might very properly designate as "the Age of Letters" or pictorial writings such as the rock carvings of Upper Egypt. All these comprise that transitional period, dim memories of which lingered on well into historic times.

These were ages of popular myths, folk-lore, demi-gods, eponymous heroes, traditions of actual happenings, and philosophic theories on Man and his surroundings. From the vast materials thus supplied poems were afterwards written, new religions were founded, and later lawgivers came into existence.

In China early historians still remembered the even more remote "Age of the Three Rulers," when people subsisted on wild fruits, uncooked food, drank the blood of other animals, lived in caves and wore for clothing the skins of wild beasts (New Stone Age). "Then came beneficent rulers who introduced orderly government, organized society on the basis of marriage and family, invented nets and snares for fishing and hunting, taught the people to rear domestic animals and till the land, established markets for the sale of farm produce, explained the medicinal properties of plants, studied astrology if not astronomy, and appointed 'the Five Observers of the Heavenly Bodies' (our Prehistoric Age)," says Keane.

The back-ground of sheer savagery lying behind all later cultural development is thus everywhere revealed. The "Golden Age of the poets fades with the *Hesperides* and Plato's *Atlantis* into the region of the fabulous."

The general use of letters is conspicuously the most characteristic feature of strictly historic times. This use of letters enabled the race to perpetuate everything worth preserving and has proven the most useful and fruitful of human inventions. Knowledge thus became cumulative and human progress was greatly accelerated. Our modern systems of writing have evolved from pictorial representations' of things and ideas. Following picture writing—so characteristic of early civilization in Egypt and elsewhere—came crude signs and symbols representing words which were first used in combination with pictures. Gradually the signs of words came more and more into use as the pictures fell into disuse. The Chinese early developed a very elaborate sign system in their script. Articulate sound-signs (letters), as in our own alphabet, is the recent perfecting of these various methods of recording ideas. Between these two extremes—the pictograph and the letter—there are various intermediary forms such as the rebus, the full syllable, etc.; these are largely preserved in both the Egyptian and Babylonian systems, and help to show how the pure phonetic systems were finally reached. This must have been accomplished at least six thousand years ago—probably ten thousand since its first invention—since various archaic phonetic scripts are found widely diffused over the archipelago (Crete, Cyprus, Asia Minor) in Mykaenean and Pre-Mykaenean time. The hieroglyphic and cuneiform systems from which they originated were unquestionably much older, since the rock inscriptions of Upper Egypt are pre-dynastic—prior to all historic records —while the Mesopotamia city of Nipper already possessed half-pictorial, half-phonetic documents some six or seven thousand years before the New Era. In this connection Keane says: "From the pictorial and plastic remains recovered from those two earliest seats of the higher cultures it is now placed beyond doubt that all the great divisions of the human family had at that time already been fully developed. Even in the New Stone Age the present European type had been thoroughly established as shown by the skeletal remains of the 'Cro-Magnon Race,' so called from the cave of that name in Perigord where the first specimens were discovered. A skull of the early Iron Age from Wildenrot in Bavaria had a cranial capacity of one thousand five hundred and eighty-five centimetres, and was in all respects a superb specimen of the regular-featured North European. In Egypt, where a well-developed social and political organization may be traced back to the eleventh century B. C., Professor Petrie discovered in 1897 the portrait statue of a prince of the fifth dynasty (3700 B. C.) showing regular Caucasic features. Still older is the portrait of the Babylonian King Enshagsagna (4500 B. C.), also with handsome features which might be 'either Cemitic or even Aryan.' Thus we have a documentary evidence that the Caucasic, that is the highest human type, had already been not only evolved but spread over a wide area (Europe, Egypt, Mesopotamia) some thousands of years before the New Era.

"The other chief types (Mongol, Negro, and even Negrito) are also clearly portrayed on early Egyptian monuments, so that all the primary groups had already reached maturity probably before the close of the Old Stone Age.

"But these primary groups did not remain stationary in their several original homes, but have on the contrary been subject to great and continual fluctuations throughout historic times. Armed with a general knowledge of letters and correlated cultural appliances, the higher races soon took a foremost place in the general progress of mankind, and gradually acquired a marked ascendency, not only over the less cultured peoples, but to a great extent over the forces of nature herself." Says Keane.

Now the intelligent application of the foregoing facts can lead to no other than the following conclusions: That evolution—the immutable *modus operandi* of that great Final Cause—is the real, discovered cause of every change that has ever taken place, and that this is true, not only of earthly changes, but is equally applicable to the limitless universe, co-extensive with force and space; that nature requires an almost inconceivably long time to produce even the slightest variation; that Man is the product of natural law; that the superior mental attainment of the modern European is the result of aeons of favorable environment; and by inference, that his laggard black brother is mentally thousands—if not millions —of years behind, and must needs lose out in the conspicuously unequal struggle for existence. Not only because of his mental inferiority, must the American Negro ultimately lose in this contest, but because also of strong and increasing mutual race prejudice and of his relative numerical weakness. Thus it seems to be demonstrated truth that while remotely we started out in an ape-like form and on equal footing, natural law has so favored certain branches of this human family-tree as to cause them to develop out of all proportion to certain other branches; just as we see illustrated, every day of our lives, in the development, and lack of development, in different branches of ordinary trees.

CHAPTER II

The Natural Moulding of the Races From a Common Prototype

WE have seen then that Man is only one of the many natural products of orderly change constantly going on about us, and that he has been gradually elevated by imperceptible changes from lower forms. Likewise it has been shown that while his nearest prehuman ancestors were not existing apes they were common ancestors to both Man and ape, and very much closer in form and appearance to present-day apes than to the higher races of Man. As the progeny of this common ancestor have diverged, and finally become so widely differentiated as to constitute a number of separate and distinct species, so each of these latter in turn—under the same fixed law—exhibit this tendency to divergence, including Man himself. Hence the existence upon the earth to-day of the many and widely different types or varieties of the human race. For thousands of years, perhaps it is well within the bounds of conservatism to say hundreds of thousands of years, after the landed portions of the globe became peopled all men were still very much alike; and all were somewhat inferior, *mentally,* if not *physically,* to even the lowest existing types. If during the last two or three thousand years progress and development and ready means of inter-communication had not taken place, but instead the several grand divisions of land had permanently remained isolated, and if this condition could have extended indefinitely into the future, the several varieties of Man, or some of them, would ultimately have developed into distinct species—a remoteness of relationship sufficient to prevent inter‑ breeding. In many respects it seems regrettable that it did not so happen, for it would have been interest‑ ing to have had a free exchange of ideas and com‑ modities with a people, possibly our full equals, but with whom our blood would not have mixed. As a matter of fact, however, if extensive racial reversion is impossible and modern progress and intercourse continue, the many varieties of mankind must con‑ tinually approach closer and closer to a common type. This will take place very gradually of course, but will be much faster than most of the evolution‑ ary changes of the past have been.

In the beginning, as we have shown in the last chapter, Man was the natural product of common ancestors, and consequently they were all of the same variety. The wide variations that have since taken place are the results of respective environ‑ ments, and if such environments and isolations had continued indefinitely they would unquestionably have produced new species as we have said. The progress of this primitive Man from his tropical birthplace to the remote, and even frigid regions of the earth, both north and south, was necessarily dif‑ ficult and slow; all routes were beset with obstruc‑ tions and he had nothing to facilitate his journeyings except his bare feet and grasping hand, with oppos‑ able thumb. But this peopling of the earth, slow as it must have been, was fast when compared with the laws of adaptation. Consequently, while we have the best of evidence that it required many thousands of years for the primitive race to occupy all the principal landed portions of the earth, it is equally well established that evolution required millions to differentiate him into the various groups, or races, as they exist to-day.

It is, however, no easy matter to convince the mass of the people, who have had little or no scientific training, that there was a time when all human beings were as much alike as are the members of a native Sudanese tribe, but it is none-the-less true. The greatest single obstacle in the way of popular advancement along such lines, is the eagerness and energy, with which both the politician and the theologian seek to make capital out of the situation. We once heard a famous politician preach a political sermon which he entitled "The Prince of Peace" in which he went out of his way to introduce the false statement—but popular belief—that modern science made the claim that human beings were nothing but improved, present-day monkeys. He said to his immense audience, in effect, that such claims were both disgusting and insulting, that he, for one, did not believe them and that he preferred to hold to the teaching of the Bible on the subject. Continuing he said, that it was much more likely that monkeys are degenerate men than that men are improved monkeys; and to his mind the latter was a far more plausible theory. Of course this brought him loud applause from an audience composed largely of uncultured people, which he carefully sized up before making the misleading and ridiculous statement. We observed him as he stood silent for a moment, evidently considering how many votes he had probably made by this shameful sacrifice of honesty and truth.

Theologians are constantly misleading the people in a similar manner, but we will modify our criticisms so far as they are concerned, giving them the benefit of the doubt, and supposing that, on their part, such false impressions are made only through ignorance and superstition.

A more important consideration for our purpose, is how the several divisions of mankind came to be so unlike, and the causes that have contributed to these morphological distinctions.

The power of analogy to reveal the truth is often more reliable than direct testimony. Such is pre-eminently the case when we come to deal with great questions of past causes and effects. This very matter of the development of the several races could now be demonstrated by such abstract reasoning; but fortunately the anthropologist is ready with his direct and positive proofs, in the form of fossil remains, to verify the work of the philosopher.

As we have seen in the preceding chapter the human race was evolved or born in or near the island of Java, certainly within eight degrees of the equator, where luxuriant vegetation and aqueous animals furnished an abundant supply of food. This primitive Man, however like his simian ancestors, must have been very largely a vegetarian. But natural law had foreordained that the race should not always be confined to this tropical region of lassitude and plenty. The majority were contented, just as certain lower races still are, with a simple life of comparative idleness. We can imagine these rude ape-like men in the hot sunlight and under the great spreading palm trees along the waters edge contented with the daily gratification of the animal appetites—lacking incentive and stimulation to a higher mental plane. But in fulness of time they developed their restless, ambitious spirits, who longed to know more of nature and her wonders; willing to risk their lives and brave the hardships of colder, and apparently less favorable climes in order to gratify the yearnings of their more active minds.

Thus of course, the adventuresome spirits who went out from among their fellows, seeking new environs and strange abodes, were drawn from the most active and enlightened stratum of this simple stock. He was the elect of his race; more capable of protecting himself against his many new dangers.

We also have good reasons for believing that this primitive Man was none too choice about the source of his food supply, and that a member of a hostile tribe, when slain or captured was eaten raw and relished. Nor is it likely that he would hesitate, when pressed by the pangs of hunger, to put the peaceful but weaker members of his own tribe to a similar use.

It is not easy to appreciate in our present state of development, with every mechanical need anticipated and abundantly supplied in every relation of life, with articles well-nigh perfect for the purposes intended, how difficult it was for this rude man to procure the simplest articles of utility and warfare. For instance if he had been furnished with a single mechanical aid to the power and effectiveness of his arm, such as the ordinary baseball bat, his ability to make war upon other tribes, and upon the fierce animals of primeval forests, would have been vastly augmented. In the absence of any such article his ingenuity suggested that the human femur, or thigh-bone, be made to serve the purpose, and it is believed that the use of thigh-bones was in these very early stages of human existence, at once, the most common and formidable weapon at the command of the race. When these wild tribes chanced to meet in the vast unbroken forests of the age a fierce contest generally ensued; for each human body meant a good supply of food and two additional implements of warfare.

Man must have been very far above his first ancestors (Dubois's Javanese Man) before he was able to make stone hatchets, with which to hew out wooden clubs, and still more advanced when he became able to supply a sufficient number of stone implements for general utility in defensive and offensive warfare. But what we wish to illustrate is the fact that each of these stages of development raised the race in physical form by developing the levers of the body—bones, tendons, and muscles—and by improving the shape of the hands and fingers; all of which implies a corresponding improvement in the power of thought through increased use of the entire nervous system which includes the brain.

When the race had once established itself in such latitudes as Central Asia and Europe its dietary necessities were greatly changed; more heat-producing animal food and less vegetable matter was necessary. Moreover, it no longer had the variety and abundance of fruits and vegetables that nature so lavishly furnished in its equatorial habitats. In great measure the substitution of flesh for vegetable matter had become necessary and the former could be had only by effort and ingenuity. It could have been no easy matter even in these early times—when the lower animals were much more abundant than at present—for the various tribes of the primitive race to resist the cold, capture their food, and maintain themselves against hostile tribes as they penetrated deeper and deeper into the unknown wilds and frigid regions of both north and south.

We trust it has been made sufficiently clear then, that as primitive Man forced his way out from the equator his wits were continually whetted and sharpened by the very nature of his new condition. It should also be apparent that those who went out were, for reasons already mentioned, the select element mentally and physically.

These pilgrims, who braved all sorts of new dangers—thus eliminating all but the fittest—established themselves in various and sundry localities, some more suitable for racial development than others, but all better than his torrid birthplace. Those who continued to dwell in hot climates underwent little change, and all succeeding generations perpetuated this simple life and many primitive race characteristics. This is the environment that has produced the Negro race. Very slight adaptational changes have occurred in this division of the race, thus he has remained much closer to the original stock than have the higher branches of the race.

On the other hand, the constant introduction of new factors into the conditions and changing environs of the adventuresome element, caused corresponding changes in the organism, until at last, under the influences that acted upon these various roving tribes, or nations, the several principal varieties of mankind became well established.

The somewhat arbitrary classification into four great primary divisions, according to their geographical location and state of development, is by no means perfect, but is extremely useful for purposes of study, and is perhaps as good as could be made.

Thus we have the Negro race (Ethiopian) which remained permanently in hot climates and varied but slightly from primitive types. The Amerind (American Indian), who is much higher than the Negro, but not endowed with sufficient capacity to develop a great civilization, though Montezuma and the old city of Mexico indicate that if left alone long enough, the Indian would have developed a much more extensive civilization.

Next above the Indian stands the Mongol division (Yellow or Brown race). This division is
strong in every sense, with a very great and extensive civilization, perhaps the most ancient of all.
Any comparison of the Mongol with the Amerind
would be odious, since the Orientals are a highly
civilized, intellectual, and cultured people, exercising
a very great influence in the international councils of
the world. But in spite of all this the fact remains
that the Caucasian division is pre-eminently and in-
disputably superior to them all. To mention his
works and achievements is to sum up at least ninety
per cent. of all important human accomplishments.
Still we are told by many—notwithstanding these
facts—that the Negro is to be elevated and presently
to take his place as the equal of any, including our
American division of the Caucasian race. We cannot believe it. The very suggestion is preposterous.

Special adaptation to environment is seen then to
have been the author of the four principal varieties
or races of mankind.

In contemplating the relative merits and demerits
of the Caucasian and Negro races, respectively, we
must keep the great truth of causation ever before
us, remembering that there is no truth in the antiquated superstition that all things were made for
Man's pleasure and convenience, divinely ordained
to fit his needs; but, conversely that Man is a mere
by-product of natural law, and, consequently fitted
by nature to his environs, of which he is simply part
and parcel. In his present civilized condition, however, he is none too well fitted—for weaklings are
artificially preserved, and natural laws are constant-

ly violated.*

The object of this work does not justify an elaborate treatment of these subjects. Our purpose in introducing these chapters dealing with the origin of the race, and the primary divisions thereof, together with their respective mental and physical characteristics, is *solely* to show how we came by such faculties as we have, and what the Negro race lacks that the Caucasian possesses. The enormity of the intellectual and moral breach that separates these two divisions of mankind must be made plain. Having these fundamental principles well fixed in our minds we will be better prepared to consider those two divisions of the race, which natural causes and untold ages have combined to make, the one the highest and the other the lowest of the four grand divisions as they exist to-day.

LIFE AND HABITS OF PRIMITIVE MAN

Almost the entire landed portions of the earth bear witness to the life and habits of primitive Man during the ages when he was little if at all divided into varieties or races. This period, known as the First Stone Age, must have been longer than his entire subsequent history. The first rudely fashioned instruments of Man,—after the period of bones and sticks—the paraphernalia of hunting and fishing and the utensils for the preparation of food, were

---

*As we have stated elsewhere, it seems probable that present and prospective influences will ultimately bring the higher races into much closer association and make their environment so similar and their intercourse so free, that in sufficient time racial peculiarities will become much less. sharply marked if not ultimately obliterated; while the low and unfit elements will diminish and tend to disappear under the law of the *survival of the fittest.*

all crudely formed of stone and other substances. This is the immutable record of the early stages of human development. This fashioning of stone to meet his necessities constitutes a potent cause of his upward progress. A great part of the men and boys of these early times—probably women also—must have been constantly occupied in finding suitable stone beds, in quarrying, designing, and shaping the raw material into serviceable forms.

Following this age the student of Man's development notes a very decided improvement in the capacities of the race; the stone implements are better formed for the purposes intended. Their symmetry, or outlines and proportions, as well as their finish, or polish, is observed to have undergone marked improvement. This change which was not sudden, as it might appear from the context, but very gradual —covering many thousands of years—marks the beginning of the New Stone Age. Sir William Turner has estimated that this covered a span of not less than one hundred thousand years. Even this computation may yet prove to be inadequate and it would not be surprising if anthropologists of the future greatly extend the period.

Concomitant with this epoch is noted a very conspicuous improvement in the human faculty of originality, evidenced by increased ability to design as well as to execute. During this New Stone Age Man, in his respective geographic localities, became more or less differentiated into what was later to develop into the several well-defined varieties. Even if his general physiognomy was yet little removed from his primordial ancestors—characterized by the *Javanese link*— his mental powers reveal decided divergence and improvement. The Man of Spy, (unearthed in Spy in Belgium in 1884) or the Neanderthal Man, who belonged to the Swiss Lake dwellers, and had a cranial capacity of about 1033 cubic centimetres—which is half way between the present low races and the Missing Link—also belonged to this New Stone Age.

If we admit a Copper Age, as most ethnologists and anthropologists do, it immediately followed the New Stone Age, as we have seen in the preceding chapter; but we doubt the propriety, or justification, of such a division. It is true of all natural progress that there are no well-defined lines of demarkation denoting its several stages of advancement; and, as we have had occasion to remark elsewhere, such imaginary divisions are mere inventions, or arbitrary separations for convenience of study. Such divisions afford us a mental picture, as it were, of successive stages of change and development.

This Copper Age has never seemed to us justifiable. Copper was found almost in a pure state in many localities, notably in the lake regions of North America, and was also found and utilized by prehistoric Man in Europe and elsewhere; but we are persuaded by the accumulated evidence of the most thorough students that it should not be made to constitute a separate era. The latter part, if not the whole, of the Bronze or Alloy Age must have been contemporaneous with the use of pure copper. Therefore we say that the use of copper should not be made to constitute a separate period in the upward progress of the race. In many localities copper was unknown and in such lands the progress of man seems to have passed gradually from the use of stone to the use of alloy. As has been pointed out by Dr. Keane, and others, these ages overlapped one another and in many localities it is quite hopeless to attempt a separation even for convenience of study. We may correctly assume that, in a general way, the Neolithic, or New

Stone Age, immediately preceded the Copper Age—
if we admit a separate Copper Era. It is best we
believe, to make the division more general, and instead of attempting to define a separate Copper Age,
and later an Alloy or Bronze, and lastly an Iron Age,
to include the whole under the modern term—"The
Metal Ages."

The foregoing then are the principal materials
used by (so-called) prehistoric Man for weapons and
other purposes, in his successive stages of upward
progress and differentiation from a common stock or
prototype, into the many varieties which, for convenience, we have divided into four primary groups
or races. The Mongols, of which division the Chinese, Japanese, and Central Asiatics are the chief
representatives, seem for a time to have kept pace
with the Caucasians, if indeed, some ten thousand
years ago, some of them were not actually in advance
of the latter. It is highly probable that there was a
time, preceding the great civilization of ancient and
prehistoric Egypt, when the Chinese were the most
advanced of all peoples. But admitting this to be
true, under the very recent, but securely established
law of caucasion—due to influences which we know
not, or at least cannot trace—this division practically
ceased to advance. A fact due to inherent antecedent causes which, if they could be known, would
probably be found hundreds of thousands of years
prior to the dawn of history. It is not without the
bounds of possibility to suppose that the Chinese actually retrogressed during many generations, while
certain Caucasic peoples continuing their progress
became the undisputed leaders in nearly every line
of thought and progress.

From the time that Man first went out from his
primitive home, leaving behind the non-progressive,

he waged a continuous battle for existence; contending with the endless difficulties of procuring food and shelter; and doing battle with the fierce wild animals of the pristine forests, and hostile tribes of his own kind. Such adversity necessarily tended to increase his powers and to eliminate all but the fittest, both mentally and physically.

After careful study of various works on ethnology and anthropology, including Vogt, Hodgson, Nott, Keane, and others, all of whom will admit a vast antiquity for man, we are of the opinion that he has existed upon the earth even longer than any of these authorities have ventured to assert.

Basing our reasoning on data collected from all branches of science that can be made to contribute either directly or indirectly, we would give it as probable that our earliest upright ancestors (Pithecanthropus Erectus) lived as long ago as twenty million years, and that the Old Stone Age probably had a duration of not less than five hundred thousand years. The second, or New Stone Age, while shorter, must have covered at least one hundred thousand years. Since the close of the two Stone Ages there is no means of accurately estimating the milleniums that passed during which Man used principally copper, pottery, wood, various alloys of metal (generally known as bronze since they usually contained copper), and finally Iron. Of course there were no well-defined lines, marking these several periods, as we have already seen; Man in his different modes of life and in the several broad areas of his domestication, varied greatly in his daily life as well as in the substances or materials utilized.

Coming back again then to the probable causes of the differentiation of mankind into the primary races, or varieties (four in our division), let us take a final

survey: Why are the lowest varieties black, Doli-
chocephalic (long-headed), prognathous (slanting
teeth and protruding jaws), with thick inverted lips,
nappy or wooly hair, and flat noses? And why, on
the other hand, are the highest varieties white usually, Brachycephalic (round-headed), with small
jaws, perpendicular teeth, thin lips, straight or curly
hair, and small high noses? In our judgment, no
positive assertions regarding the exact details are
justified by the evidence thus far adduced; but we can
say, in a broad general way, that climate, environment, and aeons of time have most assuredly done the
work. The details of the many causes and effects are
impossible to trace. Moreover, there would be no
justifiable end to compensate for the infinite trouble
even if this were possible. Myriads of causes and
their effects would have to be traced through millions
of years—clearly an impossibility. But to the impartial observer, the superiority of the Caucasian, or
white races, is so constant and overwhelming that
further argument or citation in this connection is
wholly unnecessary. The subject of mental inferiority of the Negro will, however, be taken up in a
separate chapter and treated in a more exhaustive
manner.

Ethnologists and anthropologists are very uniformly agreed that the north of Africa—that portion
lying between the Sudan and the Mediterranean—is
most likely the pristine home of the white race. This
is the only element of truth in the absurd hypothesis
of Dr. Scholes (to whose writing we refer in the
fourth chapter of this work), that the Caucasian is
merely a white-skinned Negro.

All evidence which we possess points strongly to
the conclusion that Man has inhabited this region
from time immemorial (in late Pliocene or early

Pleistocene times), when the species was little if at all differentiated into races, and that it was probably in this locality that he developed into the Caucasic type. This, however, is by no means positively established, although we see no objection to the theory, since it is proven truth that the earliest specimens of the genus were necessarily alike and that during untold ages in some locality, or localities, as the case may be, certain descendants of this rude first Man developed by imperceptible change into our finest European type. All that has been said on the subject of races goes to prove that we Caucasians are brothers of the Negro, since we all came from a common stem; but to illustrate the absurdity of the claim of close relationship, it may be said with equal truth that in still earlier zoological ages our ancestors came from marsupials and further back still from fishes. Those who make such claims might well add that naturalists generally would support the statement that among our sufficiently remote ancestors may be counted the kangaroo, the opossum, and the fishes that swim in the sea.

There is no objection to the theory that the highest type of the human family was evolved somewhere in that vast section of the African Continent lying north of the seventeenth degree of north latitude, or even north of the tropic of Cancer, as seems to be the concensus of opinion of those best qualified to judge; yet we do not consider that it is a matter which can be positively ascertained at the present time. If we were called upon to pass judgment independently upon the evidence and were unaware of such eminent ethnologists as Keane, Deniker, Much, O'Schrader, Sergi, and others, in favor of the north of Africa, we would as soon believe that the Caucasian, or Aryan peoples had their primitive home

in what is known as the Pamitian region of the Hin-
du Kush, or somewhere between the Caspian and the
North Seas, or rather in the Steppe Land of southern Russia, as elsewhere stated. This again, however, is a matter of no particular importance or bearing on the relations of the races, or the Negro question. Keane himself makes this admission of uncertainty: "To the question where was the Caucasian
type constituted in all its essential features, no final
answer can be given; but it may be confidently stated
that Africa north of the Sudan corresponds best to
all the known conditions."

The Aryan is a very ancient inhabitant of both
Asia Minor and Central Asia. In the culture of
Asiatic Peoples, especially Southern Asiatics, the
Aryan element is old and far-reaching. It is commonly supposed that what is now the Sahara, or
Great Desert, was a marine bed during that vast
period of the differentiation or natural moulding of
the races; but quite the contrary is now known to be
true. All of the north of Africa was then well
watered and fertile. The climate was almost ideal,
every physical condition for great specialization was
presented, such as ample space, abundance of food,
and favorable climate. There were three continuous land connections across the Mediterranean,
which enabled African fauna to move with perfect
freedom between the two continents—Africa and
Europe.

One of the strongest arguments in favor of the
north of Africa as the scene of extensive improvement in the primitive race, and the birthplace of the
Caucasic division, is the knowledge that the greater
part of Europe was exposed to glacial invasions, and
was largely covered at long intervals by successions
of ice-caps. For many thousands of years—during

which Europe was repeatedly devastated by glaciers —the vast Sahara region presented an almost ideal climate. So far as climate is concerned this region is believed to have been Utopian, and recent investigations have demonstrated that it was the continuous home of Man during a very long prehistoric age. It is certain that he here underwent great changes and improvements both mental and physical. The present arid wastes of the Sahara district were once traversed in all directions by splendid water-courses, such as the Igharghar river flowing north into the Mediterranean and the Massarawa, which found its outlet into the Niger after watering a magnificent country as it wound its way to the south. It is scarcely necessary to mention that there was no lack of animal and vegetable life in a land so highly endowed by nature with every requisite for their sustenance.

In addition to these advantages this Sahara district enjoyed the tempering climatic influence of cooling breezes from the north during the ice invasions in Europe together with an average elevation of more than one thousand feet above sea level.

Many eminent authorities believe that this is the land where the rude wandering tribes of primitive Man, after a residence of hundreds of millenniums, developed into the race which later stocked the greater part of Europe and which we know as the Caucasian or Aryan type. All these advantages of the north of Africa are clearly pointed out by Keane in his two works—"Man Past and Present," and "The World's Peoples."

This is the race which has produced nine-tenths of the great men in the world's history. Likewise it has originated the greatest civilizations of both ancient and modern historic times. To it the other three great divisions of mankind are indebted for nearly every notable invention and discovery, which in late centuries have come to us so continuously that a review of even the more wonderful and conspicuous examples would read like a fairy tale.

We have spoken briefly of the causes which have contributed to make the black man what he is as well as those that have produced the white man. A volume could very easily be written on this interesting subject, but the work before us does not admit of greater elaboration. To those who are not broadly acquainted with science and philosophy, especially the physical sciences, such as geology, zoology, botany, chemistry, and the rest, but who, nevertheless desire to enter more deeply into the great truths here briefly outlined, we can only commend the exercise of common sense, or the use of ordinary judgment and reason in connection with their studies, for none of us can be well versed in all branches of knowledge. For instance, the author of this work is compelled, through ignorance, to accept the statements of astronomers for the correctness of their calculations in higher mathematics. The careful study of a few great works—such for instance, as Herbert Spencer's "First Principles of Philosophy;" John Stuart Mill's "System of Logic;" Huxley's "Man's Place in Nature;" Darwin's "Origin of Species," and "Descent of Man," will prove of great benefit to any who would know better the vital and fascinating questions of the moulding of the races and the development of the higher mental faculties. The deepest questions concerned in the consideration of our Negro Problem are those of cause and effect, and especially inherited qualities and tendencies. How often we see superficial articles in periodicals written by people who, for one reason or another, have gotten their names before the public, but for the most part are obviously and sometimes painfully ignorant, or unmindful, of the great truths of science and philosophy, which so clearly must form the basis of all intelligent efforts to presage the ultimate destiny of the Afro-American Negro.

CHAPTER III

Native African Peoples

IT is by no means true, as many seem vaguely to suppose, that—when Egypt is excepted—the Dark Continent is practically the exclusive domain of the Negro race. In addition to the very many tribes and varieties of savage and barbarian black men, there are, and always have been, important indigenous African white or Caucasic races. Despite the fact that these ethnological questions are fraught with interest, they are peculiarly seductive; and when once we allow ourselves entangled in their meshes escape is well-nigh impossible. However, we cannot evade the danger altogether, since the reader must have some outline of the relations of the African Negro tribes—from which our American stock was largely drawn—to their Caucasic neighbors.

The most widely accepted theory of the formation of the Caucasic race—for it is but a theory—is that it was first formed from the primitive stock somewhere in the north of Africa; probably in that vast plateau which at present consists of arid sand wastes, —the great desert of Sahara—for, as we have seen elsewhere, this was certainly one of the most favored regions of the earth during hundreds of thousands of years. This white, or Caucasic people early became differentiated into two famous subdivision: the Semites and the Hamites. The Semitic branch is supposed to have subsequently passed over the Red Sea into Arabia, there to become still further specialized and to have given off various tribes into

47

other portions of Southwestern Asia; for the Semites who went out from Africa to constitute these races or varieties, are supposed to be the indigenous race of Arabia and certain other parts of Asia. The Hebrews or Jews, perhaps the most versatile of mankind, are also said to be a branch of this Semitic race. The Arabs of North Africa are likewise a Semitic people sent back again from Asia to the land of their earliest nativity.

The Hamites, notwithstanding various interminglings with other peoples, constitute the greater part of the inhabitants of North Africa; including the ancient Egyptians.

The Negro is widely distributed over the African continent, his domain extending from the northern boundary of the Sudan to the Cape of Good Hope, and is as broad as the continent itself; while in the southern hemisphere, and close about the equator, the region of his habitation almost encircles the earth. We are not to deal with him thus widely, however, for his principal numerical strength and purest type are to be found in the Sudan and the territory to the south of it. In that continuous region bounded on the north by the northern boundary of the Sudan; on the east by the Red Sea, the Gulf of Arden, and the Indian Ocean; and on the west by the Atlantic Ocean, are to be found more than one hundred million Negroes. It was from the savage and barbarian tribes of the western portion of this vast region that our American slave stock was principally drawn.

The Hamitic and Semitic peoples are believed to have originated in the region of the Sudan immediately adjacent to the Negro domain and with overlappings at certain points. If such be the case it is inconceivable that intermingling of blood along the border line should not have taken place.   In fact it is quite clear that this mixing of blood has taken place to some extent.   The ancient Egyptians had a slight strain of Negro blood in their Hamitic veins, and in many of the border tribes of African Negroes both Hamitic and Semitic strains can be traced. Some writers have tried very ingeniously to make it appear that this intercourse and intermingling of blood has been sufficient in the past to greatly improve the Negro intellect and character, but a moment's reflection will suffice to show the absurdity of this.   In the first place ready means of communication was not to be had in these early times, and where civilized peoples bordered on the territory of a lower race a state of hostilities perpetually existed; both of which causes tended to limit the mutual diffusion of blood.   Then, too, it has been demonstrated that where such admixture takes place between varieties there is a constant tendency toward a return to a pure type in the direction of a preponderance of a given blood.   In other words if a human mongrel produced by the admixture of white and Negro blood is less than half white its progeny has a natural tendency to revert to a pure Negro stock.   For instance, if the Hamitic and Semitic admixture had caused the entire Negro population of Africa to become one-third white when the supply of white blood was shut off it would finally have returned to the pure Negro type.   As a matter of fact this white blood-supply has never amounted to one thousandth part of this indigenous Negro race.   In most instances the American supply of African Negroes were free from even this insignificant cross-breeding. The West Coast Negroes, from whom our American stock was chiefly drawn, are the peoples we are to consider in this chapter.

A little more than twenty-four centuries ago the historian Herodotus explored the west coast of Africa and penetrated the country to a considerable extent. As a result of this he tells us that, in addition to Phœnician and Greek intruders there were two distinct indigenous peoples, the Libyans (Hamitic), in the north and Ethiopians (Negroes), in the south. The ethnical divide between the Libyans and Ethiopians may be roughly indicated by drawing a line across the continent seventeen degrees north latitude.

In the preceding chapter the peculiar physical characteristics of the Negro have been outlined. Among the more notable variations of this type may be mentioned the Bantu, and the Bushman, or dwarfs. The Bantu is distinguished by certain slight modifications of the Sudanese type. The face of the Bantu is certainly less coarse than that of the Sudanese; it may indeed be regarded as relatively refined. The jaws are less projecting and the lips noticeably thinner. In stature the Bantu corresponds with the Sudanese quite accurately, while in color he exhibits all shades of dark brown but is rarely strikingly black. These Bantu tribes are found southward from the Sudan to the Cape. While as we have noted, this variation of the Sudanese Negro— the Bantu—presents many slight variations, his chief distinguishing quality is *linguistic* rather than *physical.*

The other chief division of this Sudanese stem is a people of peculiar interest; so extraordinary indeed as to justify some mention. We refer to the African pygmies, or dwarfs. These little people are almost as wild as lower animals, and make their home in the dense and inaccessible forest lands. Historic writings of these little folks—averaging four feet high—seem to tax the credulity of many readers, but there is no better authenticated fact in history than the existence of this extraordinary subdivision of the species. This dwarf division of the Sudanese Negroes may very properly be regarded as the true aborigines of Central Equatorial Africa. In the earliest (Pharoahonic) times—we might also say in prehistoric times—these Central African dwarfs were not only known to the Egyptians but were also highly prized at the courts of Europe.* Keane states that they probably pentrated, during *Neolithic* times into Central Europe; an opinion founded on most substantial evidence.

Securely-authenticated history records the fact that as long as four or five thousand years ago these pygmies of Central Africa found their way down the Nile valley into Egypt. Keane also states that the frequent reference to them in "The Book of the Dead"†

---

*Dwarfs, and stories of dwarfs, have for all historic time been matter of peculiar and fascinating interest to young and old, layman and scientist, alike. Our literature, teeming as it does with fictitious writings on the subject, seems to have produced a widespread skepticism. But here, as is usual, there is a sound background of fact. In addition to the numerous tribes of indigenous dwarfs (denizens some hold them to be—but erroneously we think) inhabiting the tropical forests of Africa, there are others, such for instance as the Adamen Island dwarfs and the Philippine Island dwarfs. The English tradition of a race of brownies is now believed by ethnologists to be securely founded in the actual existence of an aboriginal race in those islands—a dark race of dwarf people.

†This "Book of the Dead" is most interesting. Throughout all historic Egypt it seems to have been their custom to place a book, or writing in, or near, the coffin of the dead. Sometimes this roll of papyrus was neatly packed in the armpits. The contents of these guide-books—as we may very correctly call them—varied considerably; some were more elaborate than others, especially is this true in the more recent Dynasties. The object of this book was to guide the departed spirit to what they call "The Up-

is the best of evidence that they were known to the Egyptians as early as the Sixth Dynasty.

These curious little folks were in high request at the courts of the Pharoahs in mediaeval times. The Pharoahs sent expeditions into what was known to them as the fabulous regions of Shade Land beyond Punt, to fetch and present these curiosities at court. It is therefore highly probable that during the New Stone Age these little people were frequent visitors to prehistoric rulers of Egypt.

Certain ethnologists speak of these dwarf tribes of the Sudanese Negroes as denizens of the woodlands of Tropical Africa, but it is far more correct to regard them as indigenous to the forests of this locality; for it is quite impossible, as we have shown, to prove that there ever was a time, since the formation of the races, when they did not reside therein.

The Carthaginian Admiral Hanno, who visited the west coast of Africa, somewhat earlier than did Herodotus, perhaps more than twenty-five centuries ago, speaks of this dwarf race as little hairy people seen by him.

Four feet is the average height of these curious little human beings. Their color is mostly light yellow; and, as strange and improbable as it sounds, those who have seen them describe them as covered with a sort of down. (Their skins are probably more or less uniformly covered with hair both thicker and finer than that of the white man).

---

per World" and incidently they often included hymns to appease the gods.

The individual chapters are said to bear widely different dates, most of which come down from the time of the building of the pyramids; and some are absolutely prehistoric. These ancient peoples did not call these writings "The Book of the Dead" as we do, but, "The Book of Coming Forth in the Daytime."

The hair of the head is described as crisp and of a rusty brown color.

There are also other Negro dwarf peoples, notably the Australian Black Man, which is the most inferior of all Negro races, and therefore the lowest of human kind.

It is not with these little black people, however, that we are most directly concerned; for the Negro slaves imported to America from Africa were intended to lighten, or altogether remove, the burden of hard labor from the shoulders of the Anglo-American colonists; and for such a purpose dwarfs were not acceptable to the slave-trader.

The true type of West African Negroes, as well as that which constitutes its greatest numerical strength, is tall with long and rather slender arms and legs; in this as in all other ethnical branches of the true Negro type the calves are very poorly developed, and some declare them to be absent. To these features we may add the rest that distinguish the Negro from the Caucasian.

In the foregoing pages we have shown that the Negro race has not been free from more or less contact with white races at any time, either in recorded history or in prehistoric times. And it would be a most natural inference for those not familiar with biology and the laws of cross-breeding to conclude that what was once the lowest branch of the race has, or may have, become greatly modified and improved by the admixture of white blood and other benefits of contact with white peoples. This reasoning, however, is not well founded.

The vast African territory, consisting of practically all Central, Equatorial, and Southern Africa —sometimes called Negro Land, though this term is now much restricted in virtue of the encroachment of the Caucasian on every side—was occupied for countless generations by many varieties of almost pure-blooded negroes. Up to the seventeenth or eighteenth century, of our Christian era, the conditions were such that even the higher Caucasic races could reside close together with little or no change in their racial qualities. This was especially true of a higher race in close contact with a lower one. A typical case was that of the Hamites and Semites dwelling side by side, as it were, with the Negro. The two white races preserved their respective characteristics almost as successfully as if they had been separated by unnavigated seas. The only real barriers to amalgamation were political, racial, and cultural. Race-feeling in those days was even stronger than it is at present, hard as it is for some Southerners to appreciate this. They were proud that the were not like others, that their languages were different, and that they had different methods of attaining similar ends. Then too, the Caucasic races in these early times were under the ban of religious superstition to a degree very difficult for modern men to appreciate. The dominating spirits in each race verily believed that their religion was God-given—the only true one—and that all others should be blotted from the face of the earth. All these things, as well as the total absence of modern progress and invention, which have made inter-communication so desirable and inevitable, held apart even the most enlightened peoples and caused them to treat with both fear and scorn the black, savage, pagan tribes of the unknown and perilous wilds of Negro Land.

Occasional captures of these savages no doubt were constantly taking place by both Semites and Hamites, and later by the Egyptians and other Afri-

can white peoples; and at such times women were
certainly subjected to the sexual gratifications of
their white masters. It is reasonable also to suppose that white criminals and escaped white slaves
frequently penetrated the Negro domain. And no
doubt Negro savages sometimes kidnapped their
white neighbors, but these interminglings were very
trifling when we remember that ancient Negro Land
had a population of many millions. Moreover, as
we have pointed out elsewhere, the tendency of a
race or stock to purify itself must not be lost sight of
—a race or variety constantly tending to revert to
the side of preponderance of blood. When such
admixture is arrested its effects are in time eradi-
cated.

The occupation of Africa by the Negroes took
place not later than Pleistocene times (several millions of years ago). Modern ethnologists have
thoroughly established the fact that in all essential
qualities the race seems to be practically changeless.
This grand division of mankind seems to be totally
incapable of development in any marked degree,
even when brought in close and intimate contact with
the European. Some authorities have expressed the
conviction that when left entirely alone his tendency
is toward a reversion to primitive Man if not actually to lower forms. Sir H. H. Johnson,* whom we
have quoted elsewhere, believed that the lower
tribes of Central Equatorial Africa would in time

---

*In an elaborate book recently published—which seems to have
been inspired—entitled "The Negro in the New World," this author practically repudiates all of his former writings and teachings on this subject, and gives the impression that he believes
the American Negro is a very intellectual race and that he is
even now capable of taking first rank among the most enlightened
peoples of the world. This, of course, in our judgment, greatly
lessens the value of his former statements which we have quoted.

revert to lower forms. Such slight progress as certain of these African Negro peoples have made, is without exception, the direct result of foreign influence.

It should be mentioned, however, in justice to the present-day African Negroes, that many of them have developed into herdsmen, and more or less successful agriculturists, under the influence of Hamatic, Anglo-Saxon, and other Caucasic peoples about them. Through the infusion of Caucasic blood, in such limited localities as this has taken place to any considerable extent, these Negroes show decided characteristics and tendencies of the Hamitic race.

As we have shown elsewhere, this prehistoric Hamitic race, which has penetrated certain portions of the Sudan and so greatly influenced the life and customs of certain Negro tribes—by precept, example, and interbreeding—are also progenitors of the ancient Egyptians. Thus we establish a real blood-relationship between an historic people of great culture and achievement, and a certain limited portion of this Negro race. This kinship—both slight and remote—is certainly of no importance in relation to the teeming millions of these savages and barbarians. When we remember that Africa alone—south of the Sahara and exclusive of Madagascar—has a Negro population variously estimated to be from one hundred million to one hundred and eighty million souls, or twice that of Continental United States, it is not surprising that Caucasic admixture has been of little ethnic consequence. The great mass of the Sudanese people are a pure stock and but slightly if at all removed from abject savagery. They, in common with the various tribes to the South are pagan cannibals, showing little or no capacity in their native state, for progress of any kind. Their language or various agglutinated languages, are strictly indigenous and bear little or no known relationship to the several European and Asiatic tongues.

The Cephalic index (cranial cubic capacity) of these Negro tribes varies considerably, but on the whole may be said to average about fifteen per cent. less than that of Asiatics, and a somewhat greater discrepancy exists between it and the higher European types.

The Bantu Negroes, from whom our American stock was chiefly drawn, occupy the west coast districts of Central and Southern Africa. This subdivision of African Negro races is characterized by both physical and linguistic differences. The most marked physical distinction is to be found in a general softening of the facial features; while their poorly developed language is mostly tribal or racial, it is somewhat mixed with foreign languages in certain localities. This Bantu language—if it is sufficiently developed to be called a language—is slightly if at all related to that of the Sudanese, and quite different among the many tribes.

When we enter deeply into the subject of African tribal tongues they are found to be so numerous, so ill-defined, and so imperfect that we are liable to become irretrievably entangled in a hopeless mass of savage dialects. In this matter of Negro languages there is but little distinction to be made by ordinary observers, and for the purpose of determining the state of development of the race, from which our American Negroes were largely drawn, they are of little practical use. They testify very emphatically, however, to his total lack of culture. The linguist, whose purpose and profession it is to trace and record the many rude forms of speech, and their distinguishing qualities, cannot be closely followed in these matters.

"In all the Negro lands free from foreign influence," says Keane, "no true culture has ever been developed, and here" (speaking of Africa), "cannibalism, witchcraft, and sanguinary customs are either still rife, or have been but recently suppressed by the direct action of European administration."

In the execution of our determined purpose to hew straight to the mark, in all matters of fact, and to admit nothing that savors of bias or prejudice to befog these pages, we are forced to affirm that little trustworthy evidence can be found to substantiate any claim of advancement or development on the part of the unaided Negro race.   Conversely a superabundance of the most reliable evidence is at hand to demonstrate his utter helplessness and hopelessness in his native state, when bereft of the uplifting influences of Caucasic domination. Those best qualified to judge are almost universally agreed, that,—left to his own devices—in his present physical environment, the Negro is absolutely incapable of substantial progress. Sir H. H. Johnson, to whose writings we have elsewhere referred, says, "He is a fine animal who in his wild state exhibits a stunted mind and a dull content with his surroundings, which induces mental stagnation, cessation of all upward progress, and even retrogression towards the brute." "In some respects," says Johnson, "I think the tendency of the Negro for several centuries past has been an actual retrograde one.   As we come to read the unwritten history of Africa by researches into languages, manners, customs, traditions, we seem to see a backward rather than a forward movement going on for some thousand years past—a return towards the savage and even the brute. I can believe it possible that, had Africa been more isolated from contact with the rest of the world, and cut off from the immigration of the Arab and the European, the purely Negroid races left to themselves, so far from advancing towards a higher type of humanity, might have actually reverted by degrees to a type no longer human." Keane, who quotes this statement from Johnston—in his "World's Peoples"—says of it: "I do not say that this is so, but I give it as the mature opinion of an administrator, who has had a wider experience of the natives of Africa than almost any man living."

In speaking of the Sudanese and Bantu Negroes collectively, Keane says: "Both represent various phases of barbarism, which nowhere rise to the lowest standards of civilization, but in many places present the aspect of sheer savagery, as seen in the generally hard treatment of the women, the undeveloped moral sense, cannibalism still prevalent over wide areas, the cruel practices associated with ordeals and witchcraft, the complete lack of science, letters, and stable political institution beyond the established or traditional tribal laws and customs, and more especially the arrested growth of the mental faculties after the age of puberty."

The various branches of this Bantu division inhabit the west coast districts from the Sudan to the Cape.

While ethnologists have established these two grand divisions—the Sudanes and the Bantu—they confess the distinguishing qualities to be relatively slight, and admit both to be true representatives of the lowest of the four grand divisions of mankind. The evidence presented, apart from any personal convictions of the author, is quite sufficient to show that the true Negro race is not naturally qualified for intelligent self-government. To contend as some writers have done—Scholes, for example—that the British authorities in British Africa should confer on the natives all the civil and political prerogatives possessed by British denizens, is decidedly unreasonable. A higher race cannot, by education or legislation, confer upon a lower the mental and physical qualities by which nature has foreordained the one to be the higher and the other the lower. African Negroes frequently revert to arboreal habits of life; and it has been shown in other parts of this work that mental development is arrested at puberty, and that cannibalism is at this very time rife except where it has been forcibly suppressed by Caucasic domination. Is this condition fixed by inheritance, or is it due to temporary circumstances and subject to more or less sudden and complete reversal? Is the Negro capable of sudden mental development? Throughout the nineteenth century this subject has been one of heated debate by all English-speaking peoples, nor has it been one whit lessened by the advent of the twentieth century. Most of the writings intended for popular consumption have emanated from prejudiced sources, the very bias of the individual usually constituting its inspiration—some of these writings being bitterly against the Negro, and others as strongly for him.

When the subject is calmly considered the only logical conclusion to be drawn is that the higher mental qualities are not to be suddenly acquired by any ingenious devices or processes of education. The deficiencies of the Negro are racial, deep-rooted, and of long standing.

They are the accumulated effects of adverse circumstances during thousands of generations. No earthly power can suddenly change these natural truths, "And which of you," sayeth the Book, "with

taking thought can add to his stature one cubit?   If
ye then be not able to do that thing which is least
why take ye thought for the rest?"   Time alone,
combined with ages of favorable environment, is com-
petent to advance the Negro race to that exalted position which the Caucasian now occupies.   Moreover
the competency of nature herself by long continued
favorable conditions, to bring the Negro up to the
standard of the Caucasian may well be doubted, for
we are by no means certain that the Negro type is fit
material for natural moulding into such excellencies.

CHAPTER IV

Evidences of Mental Inferiority

NOTWITHSTANDING the vast array of testimony to the contrary and singular as it may appear, there are certain authors, both American and European, who have placed themselves on record as believing that west African Negroes and their direct descendants, possess all the requisite qualities for the immediate reception of the highest Caucasic civilization and culture. In other words, and in their opinion, a certain amount of erudition can qualify these Negro peoples for the advanced thoughts and ideals of the most enlightened white races.

One of these European writers, who seems to have recently gained considerable notoriety, attempts to controvert, among a host of other securely established scientific truths, many of the chief conclusions of both Charles Darwin and Herbert Spencer. He does, however, do them the honor to apologize, in a preface to his book, for having discovered that they, among a dozen other renowned but lesser lights, were mistaken in many of their fundamental tenets. The particular author to whom we refer is one Doctor Theophilus E. Samuel Scholes (we are glad he has no other names), in his book entitled "Glimpses of the Ages," published in London in 1905. His excuse for dissenting from the deductions of these master-minds—so far as we have been able to discern—is that by some distinctively individual process of reason—we know not what—he has arrived at conclusions fundamentally different from those reached by these admitted sages. We do not know who Scholes is, but after reading his book and reflecting on some of his statements—the one just related included—we are reminded of the wit's sally who said, that, "When Bishop Berkley said there was no matter 'twas no matter what he said."

On account of the periodic circulation of such writings as Scholes's, and the further, and more important circumstance that many people well informed on other subjects have never given their attention to the sciences that have to do with the nature and development of the human intellect, it seems well to incorporate here some of the evidence which constitutes the proof that the natural endowment of these Negro peoples, when compared with the higher Caucasians, is meagre indeed, and that something more than the mere ability to imitate and copy, in a parrot fashion, some infinitesimal portion of our accumulated knowledge is requisite for the uplift of this alien and barbarous, not to say savage, race of mankind. In fact we do not believe that any material and sudden elevation by such means is possible.

In preceding chapters, which are intended to trace the descent of modern Man from his earliest human ancestors, we have had constantly in mind the necessity of impressing the reader with the almost incomprehensibly slow progress of evolutionary change; more especially is this true in the higher orders of animal life. Here again we would call attention to the fact that some millions of years have been required to raise Man from his simian ancestors to the wonderfully superior European type. The hypothesis that this has taken place in a few thousand years is contrary to the teaching of every branch of learning that has to do, even remotely, with the subject and is, of course, absurd.

It will be found upon investigation that the fabric of aggregated opinion of established authorities is well woven into the postulate, that the exalted mental equipment of the Caucasian is not to be reached by any short roads or near cuts. However, we grant that, if all other factors were equal, the stepping-stone of a vast and well-ordered storehouse of knowledge, such as the Caucasian has to offer, is, or would be, of inestimable value to any other race during that long journey from relative mental imbecility to the most superior wisdom. But alas! all things are not equal, for not only is the white man conceded to be at the top while the black man is at the bottom, but there are two other grand divisions of mankind intervening; and with them all, the freed Negro must engage in a perpetual and relentless commercial warfare for the *survival of the fittest*. Therefore we may well say that if the Negro had not this destructive warfare upon his hands, but instead possessed only the white man's accumulated wealth of knowledge and learning, together with millenniums of leisure and an all absorbing inclination towards learning and wisdom, his upward climb would not only be facilitated, but, so far as we know, assured; and the evolutionary period of incubation, as it were, would apparently be materially shortened provided, of course, that the Negro is, under any circumstances, capable of such development. Even then, when all these impossible things are granted, he would require many generations of *inherited* improvement in brain-structure, and thousands of years, to reach the pinnacle of wisdom and knowledge upon which the Caucasian stands to-day, waving the sceptre of supreme authority and dominating the habitable globe.

If it were possible to confer all these advantages upon the Negro race we would be compelled to ask and answer the question: Is the Caucasian to remain inert and stationary and wait to be overtaken; or would he continue, meanwhile, to advance as he has done in the past, and at that continually accelerated rate which is the natural consequence of powers already acquired?

Another conspicuous stumbling-block in the path of the fettered, self-constituted sociological philosopher, espousing the cause of Negro equality, is his singular confounding of *learning,* with *wisdom* or *knowledge,* and the constant mistaking of the one for the other.

No man can afford to rush into print as a teacher of philosophy who is not willing to take the trouble to discriminate sharply between these terms, which are as widely separated as the east is from the west. A man may be extensively learned and still notoriously lacking in wisdom. The one may be acquired by the individual; the other is a natural endowment. No amount of learning can produce wisdom in the lifetime of an individual, or even in a few generations; nor can the former ever be substituted for the latter. A certain amount of erudition can be acquired by members of any race, except possibly certain branches of the Negro race; but it is proverbially true that the educated fool is the most intolerable of all. On the other hand, if an individual or race is endowed with a superior intellect, his or its future is manifestly a matter only of opportunity and application. The trite expression that we cannot make a silk purse out of a sow's ear is inelegant and threadbare, we admit, but its time-worn and time-honored shell contains a rich kernel of truth.

When we begin to inquire into the abstract—an even somewhat abstruse—subject of mind, it becomes necessary to summon to our aid a little of each of the sciences of anatomy, physiology, and psychology. But we shall endeavor to clothe our thought in such simple language that all may follow closely without being conscious that we are dealing with subjects which many lay readers regard as more or less mysterious and meaningless to the uninitiated.

In all reflections upon mind we are confronted with the peculiar difficulty of the intellect, or rational faculty, attempting to observe or examine itself. However, since mind or reason is now generally admitted to be a physiological function of brain, we may attempt with some success, to comprehend the former by examining the latter.

The brain of Man is a thing of many parts and when considered in its entirety, as the central organ of the general nervous system, it becomes a very extensive and intricate subject of study. But since our purpose is only to inquire superficially into the seat and capacity for reason, this examination will be confined to the main body of the brain, or that grand division known to the anatomist as the cerebrum. The cerebrum occupies the greater part of the brain-pan, or cranial cavity, and is the seat of reason. Furthermore, it has been ascertained that the fore-part of this division of the brain, or that region known as the frontal lobes, is the portion principally concerned in abstract thought,—ideation—and that the hinder part presides over the bodily functions. This back brain is the region that contains the senses of sight, hearing, taste, touch, equilibrium, and a portion of smell, and controls the muscular movements of the body, among many other things. It was at one time believed that the cerebellum had mainly to do with these bodily functions but recent investigations has greatly modified this belief.

The front part of the cerebrum constitutes what is known as the great anterior association centre. That is to say it receives all sorts of nervous impressions or communications, both from within and without; and by some little understood functioning this heterogeneous mass of impressions—which are constantly flowing in upon this centre—are sorted out, assigned to their proper localities and, many of them, more or less permanently recorded. This is not all, they are compared the one with another, and reflected upon, and seem—in some way which we cannot yet fully explain—to give rise to new ideas. Modern physiology holds that, as a result of this process, the classified impressions act as stimuli, or excitants, to new, independent, and original ideas.

This statement may seem ambiguous and even paradoxical, and frankly we conceive it to be only a partial explanation of the workings of this highest faculty of the brain. This apparent ambiguity does not, however, militate against the grand, central, and clearly demonstrable truth, that the forepart of the brain is the seat of mentality or intellectuality. It follows therefore—other things being equal, for there are many exceptions—that a spacious forehead implies a capable machine for thought or reason.

When comparative anterior development is applied to great numbers—as ethnologists and anthropologists have very recently done in the study of races—it becomes a most valuable criterion. This method has been extensively practiced during the last few years in comparisons of the Negro with the Caucasian. Examination and measurement of thousands of disinterred crania, and of many living specimens, have revealed the fact that the capacity of the Negro skull, or brainpan, is very, materially less than that of the Caucasian.

Now there are several different methods of ascertaining the total capacity of skulls, one of these— the most commonly used—is to fill the cavity, through the *foramen magnum* (the large, round hole at the base of the skull,) with small seed and then weigh or measure the seed contained.

Measurements of this character, according to the famous ethnologist, Dr. A. H. Keane, show the average cubic contents of the male skull of the Negro races to be 1250 cubic centimetres, and that of the higher Caucasic races 1550 cubic centimetres—note the discrepancy.

Dr. Robert Bennett Bean, who contributed two able articles to the "Century Magazine" for September and October, 1896, the one on the Negro brain and the other on the training of the Negro, respectively, states that the difference in brain weight—and he weighed the brains himself of these American Negroes and whites—between the Negro and the Caucasian is about 20 per cent. in favor of the latter, which is approximately the same proportion as Keane's cubic capacity measurements given above. Moreover, the critical comparative examination of the skulls of the two races in question reveals the further, and even more significant fact, that the marked discrepancy is due *entirely* to a greater development of the front part of the Caucasian brain.

Most authorities agree that the back part of the Negro skull averages a little larger than that of the Caucasian—not only comparatively but absolutely,— and it has been observed, as this fact indicates, that the lower faculties of emotion, sight, hearing, smell, and the rest, are perceptibly more acute in the Negro; all of which is confirmatory of the argument that nature has made the reasoning part of the Caucasian brain on more liberal proportions—a fact well established by history and abstract reasoning long before we came into possession of these material evidences.

The most striking characteristics of the Negro skull are the narrow slanting forehead and broad well-rounded back head. So marked is this formation that the Negro skull is frequently described as egg-shaped with the pointed end forward. This racial characteristic is so decided and constant that medical students soon become sufficiently acquainted with it to say at once whether a given specimen is that of a Negro or Caucasian.

We have seen then that the total mass, or weight, of the true Negro brain—when dwarf races are excluded of course—averages twenty per cent. less than that of the Caucasian; that the Negro brain is both proportionately and absolutely smaller in the reasoning, forepart, and likewise larger in the back part— which latter presides over the senses and functions of the body.

Another factor of prime importance is the period at which the sutures close. The osseous shell, which incases the brain, is formed of a number of separate bones, which in childhood are incomplete, and at certain places are connected only by soft tissues. Progressive ossification from the edges of these bones gradually closes these openings by the union or joining of the several parts that are to form the fully developed skull. The object of this method of development is to allow for the growth and expansion of the brain. The complete closure of the sutures, as the anatomist would say, means, of course, the cessation of growth and expansion of the brain.

In the case of the *Negro* the sutures close completely at puberty, (sex development) about the

twelfth year, whereas, in the *Caucasian* this significant event is deferred until the mature age of forty
is reached.   It seems almost unnecessary to comment
on this bare statement of fact.   Suffice it to say that
the Negro brain is hopelessly shut off from further
development at this very early period of life; while
the brain of the white man is free to expand and
develop, as the organ becomes more and more complex, up to the fortieth year.   There is a marked tendency in Negroes of all ages to a certain gayety, fri-
volity, or childishness even under the most serious or
adverse circumstances, which is clearly traceable to
this early arrest of development—the character of
the individual remaining very much what it was at
the twelfth year.

Now we propose to show yet more clearly that
when taken in the aggregate, the character and capacity of the individual or race, are direct sequels of
the size, form, and histologic structure of the brain,
together with the blood-supply and certain other
physiological functions.   And in so far as our real
object is concerned, this demonstration may be very
largely confined to the anterior portion of the cerebrum.

Perhaps few have ever considered the bigness of
the brain of Man in its relation to the size of the
body, or as compared with the rest of the animal kingdom.   There is no other living thing—with the exception of a few of the smaller varieties of animals and
birds, and possibly certain very small insects—having
so large a brain in proportion to the size of the body,
as has Man.   He also has the largest brain—irrespective of bodily weight—of all living creatures, with
the exception of the elephant, and maybe some varieties of whales.

"History shows that the human mind, fed by constant accessions of knowledge, periodically grows too large for its theoretical coverings, and bursts them asunder to appear in new habiliments, as the feeding and growing grub, at intervals, casts its too narrow skin and assumes another, itself but temporary. Truly the imago state of Man seems to be terribly distant, but every moult is a step gained, and of such there have been many." (Huxley—"Man's Place in Nature").

All these facts go to make up collateral and corroborated evidence of the first order in support of the assertion that mass and weight of brain, when applied to whole races, or kinds, are prime factors in determining mental capacity. During the latter half of the nineteenth century, measuring human skulls with a view to determining race differences became almost a hobby; and the truth of racial preponderance of mass and weight of brain in favor of the Caucasian, as compared with the Ethiopian, was thus so securely established—with its constant twenty per cent. excess—that its successful controversion is now impossible.

But if this additional mass and weight were all—significant as is the evidence thus far adduced to show the inferiority of the Negro intellect—there are other elements that go to make up the superior brain which might yet stem the tide of scientific testimony against him. However we have no such complication to deal with, for this evidence is cumulative and the further we go with the investigation the more hopeless becomes the case of the Negro.

To repeat then what we have already stated, ideation or thought is the product of the fore-brain, and is carried on by what is known as the anterior association centre.

In order to gain a clear perception of this centre

we will liken it to a modern telephone system. The many wires and cables, or bundles of wires, which conduct the messages, correspond to the great interior mass of white brain-matter, made up of nerve fibres and bundles of fibres, the function of which is to conduct messages, or nervous impressions of all sorts, to and from the cortex, or outer surface of the brain. The telephone exchange, or central office, where these messages are first received, and where one party with a message to deliver is put into association or communication with another, who is to receive and consider the same, may be used as an illustration of the workings of the human brain.

Following the reception of such communication the latter party may ask to be allowed to confer with others, and in this way the matter in hand may be jointly considered by a large number of individuals.

This central office for connecting and associating these separate individuals, we use to illustrate the association of nervous impulses in the outer gray surface of the brain, which the latter receives by means of its lines of communication through the central mass of white matter. This process of intimate association and comparison of the many impressions there accumulated is analogous to the calling of a general mass-meeting of citizens, where all, or many important members of a community—in closer and more intimate contact—consider all the collateral evidence received by distance, or wire, communication together with a certain consciousness or judgment made up of past impressions or experiences. After this they all vote on the particular matter in hand—the minority yielding to the majority.

Processes of thought are not identical with this mass-meeting, but there is sufficient similarity in the functioning of the brain to give the reader an outline

of what takes place there during the mental operations known as the exercise of judgment, will-power,
and original ideation. This telephone system with its
central office being used for the calling of a mass-
meeting, together with the conclusions of the latter,
is relatively simple of course, but constitutes a more
or less apt metaphor. The white mass of the brain
consists of thousands of nerve fibres and bundles of
fibres for the conduction of communications to and
from the outer surface of the brain, and corresponds
to our telephonic communications.

As these impressions rush in upon this anterior
association-centre they are sorted out and referred to
sundry localities in the cortex or gray surface. Here
they are associated and compared, the one with another, and their relative importance and relationship are
believed to be passed upon by what is known as special selective cells. Many of these impressions are
then more or less permanently recorded (memory),
so that they may at any future time be called upon
and associated with both former and subsequent impressions. By means of the general nervous system
every phase of bodily sensation, as well as the entire
field of external nature about us, is constantly rushing
in upon this anterior association-centre. In consequence of the materials thus supplied and by processes which we cannot follow or completely understand, this anterior association-centre is believed to
possess the marvelous power of manufacturing new
and totally independent ideas. Were it not for this
last named faculty, the power of abstract thought,—
as the psychologist would say—education, or the acquisition of knowledge, would be of little or no use
to us. This faculty is slightly present in some species
below Man but as we descend the scale it gradually
fades away. Men who by common consent are ad-

judged fools are those who are deficient in these higher functionings of the brain. They are more or less capable of receiving and recording impressions, but unable to utilize them for the production of new and independent ideas.

Speaking collectively the Negro is known to be conspicuously inferior in this respect to the Caucasian, as all the physical evidence thus adduced would indicate. This difference is even more marked when applied to that portion of the Caucasian division of mankind known as the Anglo-Saxon, of which this American nation is largely composed. In the Negro we have shown the anterior lobes of the brain to be very decidedly smaller than in the Caucasian. The combination of a narrow anterior skull formation with a flat slanting forehead, serves to produce small and pointed frontal lobes; while those of the Caucasian are broad, high, and rounded. Thousands of recorded measurements from widely different sources bear us out in this statement.

We would call attention in this connection to the dual or multiple, nature of the evidence presented to demonstrate the mental inferiority of the Negro race. We have shown, in the first place, that the total brain weight is one-fifth less, and, in the second place, that the anterior portion—the thinking part—is, by virtue of the egg-shaped Negro skull much less developed, and that the posterior part is proportionately more developed, than is the case with the Caucasian.

But we have only begun to present the evidence at our command, that stamps the Negro as hopelessly inferior to his Caucasic brother, as regards his mental equipment. Unfortunately this evidence cannot all be introduced, and such as is must be very decidedly abridged in order to avoid, if possible, the charge of prolixity in a work designed to meet the requirements of popular reading.

However, there are certain other essential facts that cannot be omitted, even at the risk of this criticism.

CHAPTER V

Evidences of Mental Inferiority—(Continued)

REPEATED reference has already been made to the outer gray surface layer of the brain and its vital relation to the higher mental attributes. Let us examine this somewhat more in detail.

The great anterior mass of the brain, that central portion consisting of nerve fibres and bundles of fibres, for the transmission of impressions to and from the surface, is white, while the cortical surface is decidedly gray; so the former, which has to do only with the conveyance of impressions is readily distinguishable from the latter, which receives and sets in order this heterogeneous mass of nervous impulses.

What the anatomist terms the cortex, the outer gray layer, is conclusively shown to be the source of original thought; therefore it is most correctly assumed that mental capacity bears a direct relation to the development of this layer.

For the accommodation of this layer nature has made special provision. In order to confine an extensive surface layer within the limited cavity of the skull the brain is folded upon itself, the surface being thus marked by numerous elevations and depressions, the former being known as convolutions and the latter as fissures. As will be seen at once this folding serves to increase the extent of surface without actually increasing the size of the organ. Thus the number of convolutions and the depth of the fissures bear a very important relation to intellectual capacity. The complexity of this provision of nature increases throughout the scale of mammalian ascent, and attains its maximum in the most highly civilized races of Man. In conformity to this statement of fact, it has been abundantly shown by investigation that these fissures are deeper in the Caucasian brain than in the Negro brain, if indeed, they are not actually more numerous.

In order to still further increase the total amount of this gray surface matter—which increase is caused only by long continued racial use—nature has made this layer thicker throughout in the Caucasian than in the Negro race.*

If we did not possess the evidence of greater extent and greater thickness of the Caucasic brain cortex— which is abundantly shown by various authors, (see article in New International Encyclopedia on "Nervous System," among others)—the more easily verifiable truth that the total mass of brain substance is one-fifth greater in the white man, and that a very much greater discrepancy exists as regards the thinking forepart, would remain as ample proof that the Negro is mentally far behind the white man. We have never seen a direct statement on the point, but basing our estimate on various facts and figures, we should not be at all surprised if the anterior lobes of a thousand Negro brains could be weighed against the same number and same parts of Caucasian brains, if the latter were found to be very nearly twice as

*The citation of authorities and of various methods of observing these facts would unnecessarily encumber this work and obscure the object of the chapter. We are endeavoring to give the essential truths only. This is not intended to be a psychological treatise, except in so far as is directly germane to the "Negro Problem."

When there is any doubt as to the scientific accuracy of matter used, it will be given only as an hypothesis.

massive as the former.

Another essential item in intellectual acumen is cell activity. The brain cortex is made up of minute microscopic bodies called cells; the efficiency of which is partly a matter of *inherited quality,* and partly a result of *early training.* The facility with which these cells become associated, the one with another, the pair with a third and so on, is an item of intellectual ability. This faculty constitutes what is called alertness or brightness of mind as distinguished from judgment and accuracy of thought. Habit of cell-association is noticeably different in individuals and is commonly called the paths of thought.

Let us illustrate this cell-association and what is believed to occur in brain-functioning by the use of the chess-board.

To those at all familiar with this fascinating game it is scarcely necessary to state that the number of units employed as well as the spaces they may occupy are both limited, but the possible combinations and associations they may form are incalculable. This illustration may facilitate our conception of the possibilities of brain-cell association. There are only sixteen pieces used on each side in a chess game, and but sixty-four places that the men may occupy; whereas in the case of cell-association in the cortex of the brain the impulses or impressions received are incalculable, as are also the number of microscopic cells that may form combinations or associations.

This would seem to extend the power of cell-association to infinity, but experience teaches that this is not literally true; for the white man is shown by both abstract and material evidence to be vastly superior to the Negro in this respect. The activity, or alertness, of cell-association is undoubtedly a matter of inheritance to a very great extent; but we conceive that it is capable of a certain amount of improvement by intelligent early training. On the other hand we should not lose sight of the fact, in this comparison of races, that it is not possible to improve that which the individual has not inherited, and, therefore never possessed.

Here perhaps more essentially than elsewhere comes in that erstwhile mysterious factor of quality. Whether we chance to be pleased or perturbed by the eternal decree, none can deny that throughout nature there exists an unexplained difference in the organic quality of living matter. For instance, man has so far devised no means by which he can detect an essential difference in the egg, or ovum, of certain mammalian placentals; or we may take as an illustration the fœtal life of these higher animals. Up to the fifth or sixth week of this life no ingenuity of man has been able to distinguish the human from the dog or pig; yet the test of a few more weeks will show that there inheres a certain quality, or fitness —that mysterious element of kind or degree. The evidence in quality between the brain cells of the highest and lowest of human races is as positive and real, if not quite so great, as that contained in the illustration.

Then there is another factor no less significant and indeed very closely allied to the one just considered. We refer to the quality and quantity of blood-supply which the brain receives. Both common sense and established laws of physics teach us that every effect must have its antecedent cause; that there can be no production without a corresponding supply and consumption. To say that something has been produced implies that its equivalent has been consumed. The analogy is, that, a

given amount of thought produced by the brain pre-
supposes an equivalent amount of force supplied.
The blood is the source of this supply. Not only is
the blood the source of supply of energy-producing
substances to the brain, but also its only source of
elimination of waste products.

Therefore it is entirely possible for a brain to
possess all the essential qualities of fitness and yet be
totally, or largely, incapacitated by either an insufficient supply—or sluggish flow—of blood through
that organ, or by reason of a poor quality of blood
—that is, blood lacking in those elements that supply
energy to the brain.

The most expert engineer may be placed in charge
of an excellent locomotive, but without fuel it cannot
be made to turn a wheel; with an inadequate supply
it will run only feebly, or slowly, and even with an
abundant supply of inferior fuel the machine cannot
be made to do the total amount of work of which it
is otherwise capable. But if we can supply an abundance of fuel, rich in such elements as are consumed
in combustion, we get the greatest amount of work
of which the engine is capable.

Just so it is with the human brain; if its fuel,
contained in the blood-supply, is insufficient in quantity, or of an inferior quality, we do not get the full capacity of mental activity of which the machine is
capable.

The only essential difference between the engine
and the brain in this illustration is that the engine
is so constructed that its supply of fuel and its power
to eliminate its waste products are separate and distinct; whereas the brain is dependent upon the blood,
not alone for its food-supply, but for its elimination
of waste products as well.

In the comparison of the Negro with the white

man there is good evidence that the supply of blood to the brain is both greater in quantity and richer in quality in the case of the Caucasian. The brain is known to consume matter and to utilize force in the production of thought. It follows therefore, that an abundant supply of blood free from impurities, and laden with energy-producing constituents, is requisite for the best work of a given brain. Although we have little concrete evidence to adduce in this connection, analogy, or abstract reasoning, shows conclusively that there is a material difference. Certainly there is a difference in quality, and probably also in quantity, of blood supplied to the brain.

Significant indeed is the fact that the higher we ascend the scale of animal life the closer becomes the chemical and microscopic analysis of the blood. For instance, the composition of the blood of the lower varieties of monkeys is more nearly like that of Man than that of marsupials (kangaroo, opossum, etc.). Then when we come to analyze the blood of the higher apes (chimpanzie and gorilla) it is found to be so similar to that of Man that the wonder is they will not cross-breed. Even the blood-cells (corpuscles) of a dog or pig bear such close relationship, in size, shape, and number, to those of Man that it is a nice question for the microscopist to distinguish the blood of the one, from that of the other. But in spite of this extreme closeness, especially of the anthropoid apes, the fact that they will not cross-breed is evidence of a very essential difference. In view of all this we hold that—in spite of the everyday demonstration that the Negro and the white man will cross-breed—there must be an enormous difference in kind or quality of blood, producing men of such marked physical and mental dissimilarity.

This difference in quality—while not sufficient to

prevent a cross—is ample, we think, to greatly affect the character or quality of thought or ideation.

By the same process of reason, supported by incontestable evidence in the form of accomplishments, we conclude that the volume of blood-supply to the brain is greater in the Caucasian, due to better anatomical construction of the vessels and better nervous control—natural responses to long-continued exercise of a function. In other words we hold, under the general laws of evolution, that in the case of the Caucasian, who has exercised his brain for thousands of years in the higher fields of reason, there must have been some corresponding improvement in the capillary blood-vessels and their nervous supply, causing a greater volume of blood to flow through the brain, with better anastomosis and osmosis (filtration through a porus diaphragm or membrane). By this means the gray cells are more abundantly supplied with oxygen and other elements of combustion, which together supply its energy. Then, too, a greater capacity is at the same time afforded for the elimination of waste products.

As Man ascended the scale of mental development the supply of blood to the brain was increased. Both the Negro and the Caucasian have been subjected to this morphological conformity, each according to his past environment. Judging each of these races then, by its past history—a reliable criterion—we conclude that the blood of the white man is either more abundantly supplied with elements of combustion or that such elements are more accessible as a result of a more highly developed system of anastomosis and osmosis, or both.

It may be very correctly inferred from the foregoing that, we also believe, that in consequence of a more highly organized nervous system, the Caucasian is more capable of voluntary excitation of greater blood-supply to the brain for purposes of ideation; for we are very certain that such is the case.

Physiology of the human body tells us that during mental activity more than one-fifth of the total amount of blood flows through the brain.

The vasomotor nervous system of the white man is more highly developed than that of the black man. In consequence of this and other facts presented the brain of the European, or Anglo-American, is able —upon occasion of need—to demand and command a greater proportionate flow of blood to itself.

There is still another factor to be included in the evidence, which at once supports the argument already made and bears materially upon facility and clearness of thought. We refer to respiration. As every one knows the greatest energy-producer of all the elements consumed in the body is oxygen; that no combustion or liberation of energy can take place without it. This supply of oxygen is derived almost entirely from the lungs, where the minute blood capillaries receive it by osmosis. This exchange takes place through air-cells estimated to be about six hundred million in number. Likewise the blood gives off to the air in the lungs its waste products from the materials consumed in the body. We cannot enter into a detailed description of the anatomical structures here concerned, or the chemistry of the exchange that takes place. The statement that the character of the blood supplied to the brain is more dependent upon the exchange that takes place in the lungs than upon any other single consideration, must suffice.

The corollary is, that the capacity of the lungs and the delicacy, or thinness of their air-cells, together with an abundant supply and uniform distribution of capillary blood-vessels to the latter, are all factors of prime importance. That the Caucasian is superior to the Negro in each of these, every separate item of evidence which we have presented, combines to attest. The Caucasic lung capacity is ampler than that of the Negro and the facility with which the exchanges are made is simpler, owing to the more delicate structure of the tissues involved. Frederick L. Hoffman, chief statistician of the Prudential Insurance Company of America, in a work entitled, "Race Traits and Tendencies of the American Negro," presents carefully tabulated statistics showing conclusively that the lung capacity of the Negro race is materially less than that of the white man. He also holds—and offers the best of evidence to prove—that the lung structure of the white man is far less subject to diseases that impair its efficiency.

The fact that the Negro emits offensive odors, by means of the sebaceous or sweat glands of the skin, is attributed by high authorities to defective, or poorly developed respiratory organs. This, like all the evidence that has gone before, tends to show a difference in degree if not in kind, and must be imputed to the white man as an additional qualification for better cerebration. It is common knowledge among physiologists that the provisions of nature for the exchange of oxygen for waste products in the lungs are greater in the higher than in the lower animals, or races—the cells being more numerous and their structure more delicate.

In view of the enormous accumulation of direct and corroborative evidence to the contrary, the claim that the lineal and very near descendants of the African savage tribes, can in one or even a hundred generations of tutelage by Caucasians, be made equals—or anything approaching equals—of the latter race, is the most absurd. Men who make such assertions do themselves gross injustice; for one of three causes, or a combination of them all, constitutes the only hypothesis upon which their folly can be explained: They must either be adjudged ignorant of established truths, blinded with bias or prejudice; or for one or another ulterior motive, attempting to foster and disseminate doctrines which they know to be founded only in fallacy. Perhaps it is not so bad to be a fool as a knave, but since present-day knowledge places them both in the common category of natural misfortunes there is little to choose between them.

Let us then anticipate and, if possible, forestall the counter-charge that we ourselves are guilty of the shortcomings with which we charge our adversaries. Personally we would be more than delighted if in past ages natural law, or environment, had so operated as to have made the lowest of human races full equals of the highest, with all the superior mental and physical qualities possessed by the latter, even including the elimination of the carbon, or pigment, imbedded in the malpighian mucous of the skin; or, and in other words, possessed of a white instead of a black skin. But this desire can in no wise alter the facts, nor does it conform to the will of a majority of our white fellow-citizens of the South—whom we dearly love, and in many respects sincerely admire. For they possess, we think, a little more of that instinctive race-prejudice—due possibly to closer contact—which causes many of them to feel that segregation, or even extermination, would be both more desirable and more acceptable than our assent and consent to the impossible undoing and redoing of nature, in order that the Negro might not have been constituted the lowest of the races of mankind.

The modern science of ethnology divides the human species into four primary groups, or varieties, and classifies them from the highest to the lowest in the following order: Caucasian (principally European and American); Mongol (Asiatic); Amerinds (indigenous American races—commonly called Indians); and Negroes (African or Ethiopian).

We are aware of no ethnologist or anthropologist, and do not believe one worthy of the name could be found, who would not assent to the correctness of this classification, which places the Negro at the bottom and the white man at the top.

Could any thinking man with the facts before him arrive at any other conclusion? If out of such portions of the corroborative evidence as is contained elsewhere in these pages we select only that which assures us that in his native environment—unrestrained and uninfluenced by contact with higher races—he has made no upward progress from his savage condition, his assigned position, as the lowest of all races, would forever remain unassailable. Such native African tribes are to-day pagan cannibals often fattening their captives before eating; just as we fatten hogs for the same purpose. If a wife or concubine is not satisfactory, or for any caprice the man desires to substitute another, she is fattened and eaten.

In his volume of essays entitled "Man's Place in Nature" (which work is in complete harmony with what we have to say on the same subject) the late Professor Thomas Henry Huxley, the great English physiologist and naturalist, tells us that historical records show the African Negro tribes to have been the same forty centuries ago, and gives it as established truth that with the exception of such slight changes as inconceivable lapses of time will work in the most inactive, there has been no evidence of progress or mental activities during the incalculable millenniums since the slight differentiation from the earliest type of primitive Man. "Nor do the Negroes ever seem to have travelled beyond the limits of their present area," says Huxley.

It is interesting also to note that Thomas Jefferson, in speaking of the evidence of inferiority of the Negro race, and after relating with his characteristic perspicuity their notorious lack of mentality, states that it would be unfair to follow them to Africa for this investigation. Obviously this last expression was a mere figure of speech. What he meant was that the evidence of inferiority was so complete and convincing on every hand, and under his daily observation, that it was totally unnecessary to go further. But as we are treating the subject more exhaustively we have taken pains to present a certain amount of this African evidence. We consider it essential to a comprehensive understanding of our American question. It is never unfair to know the whole truth, and in dealing with the evolution of a race we can understand it best by knowing how, and under what circumstances, nature has produced it.

At the conclusion of his discourse on the Negro, Jefferson proceeds to relate the fact that the Indian, or Amerind—as we now call him—although unassociated with a superior race, developed a very considerable degree of art in engraving and carving, which he (Jefferson), very correctly we think, computes to him as evidence of superior intelligence. He concludes that the Indian is possessed of far more originality than the Negro.

However, there remains to be mentioned the fact of more or less contact and admixture of Hamitic and Semitic blood with certain of these African Negro tribes. This has gone on for a number of centuries, but when we consider the further facts that Africa is estimated to contain a Negro population of more than one hundred million, and that until very recently the greater part of that continent was a vast and practically unknown wilderness to all other peoples, laden on every hand with death to the denizen, and offering few attractions to the white man, we can readily understand that this influence has necessarily been negligible. Then, too, a preponderance of a given blood causes a constant reversion to that type in all animals and plants. For these reasons such admixture has not produced any radical change in these African aborigines. Contact with the white man, so far as it has taken place, has done more for the uplift of the Negro than has actual admixture of blood. And this is as true in America as it is in Africa. As shown in a preceding chapter, under such influences, and in certain localities in Africa, many Negro tribes have become cattle raisers and agriculturists, just as they have in America. Thus some of the tribes might more properly be called barbarians than savages, and some—under the direct influence of the white man—must be accorded the rank of civilians.

Mental faculties, whether acute or dull, are the results of causes, acting under the evolutionary law of growth and development. Cause and consequence accurately account for everything, human thought included. All we now lack—and can never fully possess—is a complete knowledge of antecedents, in order to foretell the exact result in every given case. Therefore, and while our information on these subjects is far from complete, we are able to prove *beyond question* that it has so happened that the natural law of causation has operated in the past under such *conditions,* and in such a *manner,* as to produce in the Caucasian a *brain,* or thought machine, *demonstrably superior* to that of the Negro.

This is a vast truth of nature the significance of which affords the pivotal point of the argument contained in this writing. All else is subordinate to this momentous central truth. It is at once the inspiration of the undertaking; the justification of all that has gone before; and the basis of all subsequent conclusions.

The immortal Charles Darwin taught us that under the exigencies of this universal principle the fittest only can permanently survive; and thus a great flood of light is let in upon our American Negro question the ultimate solution of which should now be manifest to all.

CHAPTER VI

Beginnings of Negro Slavery in America

WHEN slaving ships sailed from home ports for the West African coast they provided an elaborate supply of such articles as were known to lure the natives. Among these may be mentioned, alcoholic drinks, flashy articles of cheap clothing and decorations, various articles of food, and even gold coin. These wares were utilized according to circumstances; sometimes they were distributed directly and indiscriminately among the natives for the purpose of creating the impression that the white visitors were friends; again they were bestowed upon certain wicked and unscrupulous barbarians, to induce them to deliver into the hands of the donors, captives of their own race. This entering into intrigues with native chiefs and others was one of the safest and most fruitful methods of securing cargoes. A few dollars' worth of such articles as chanced to please these chiefs, or other natives, would often bring to a ship as many savages as her decks would accommodate. Sometimes these slavers would form their own marauding parties and do their own raiding in the coast country; but this was far more perilous and consequently less common. Many savages held slaves of their own, and these they were ever ready to trade and barter away for such articles as the white man had to offer. Still another practice was to send agents with trusted chiefs

into the country to negotiate directly with the natives, and to procure captives by such means as were
found to be most successful.

It will be seen that all of these methods led to the
taking and importation of the lowest and most helpless of these savages. In this way the Negroes imported into the American colonies, and later into the
United States, were almost invariably taken from
the lower strata of these savage tribes. Occasionally a *chief* was captured and delivered into the hands
of a trader by his outraged neighbors, but this was a
rare exception. Thus it is shown that the stock from
which our American Negro race was originally
drawn was not only the lowest of the four grand
divisions, but was sprung from the lower elements
of this division.

In all historic times slavery, in one form or another, has proven a constant impediment to human
progress, and a curse alike to both *servant* and *master.* At the time of the discovery of America it was
practiced and countenanced by nearly every nation
of Europe, including our English ancestors.

While Negro slave-trade was a long established
African tribal custom, foreign traffic in Negro
slaves dates from the year 1442. In that year Prince
Henry of Portugal received slaves from this source.
The European slave-trade commenced two years
later from the west coast of Africa. For half a century Portugal monopolized the trade, which finally
extended to the Spanish possessions in America.
Spain entered the trade in 1517, the English (under
John Hawkins) in 1553, and France in 1624; they
were soon followed by Denmark and Holland and
finally by the American colonies themselves. West
European countries and the Spanish West Indies

furnished a market for a time, but the Continental American colonies later became the chief outlet for the nefarious trade. England finally took the lead in this commerce, granting from the time of Elizabeth to 1670 five separate patents for its monopoly to favored merchants and companies. Between 1712 and 1749 the supply to the Spanish colonies was granted by Spain to the English South Sea Company. Gradually this commerce in human beings was extended to the Continental North American colonies in constantly increasing proportions. Of the total number of slaves imported to America (the West Indies included) previous to the American Revolution, British subjects carried more than half —employing in one year one hundred and ninety-two ships carrying four hundred and seven thousand captives. By this time the competition for the rich spoils of the traffic had become greatly diversified, and in addition to the principal maritime powers of Europe, the North American colonies themselves engaged actively in the shameful business. The principal American participants were the more progressive settlers of the North—especially Bostonians.

The practice of capture and barter in human beings should not be too severely condemned; it must be remembered that human thought and action are largely moulded by the practices and customs of the times, and that we poor mortals are not as free in our conduct as our egotistical natures incline us to believe. The great mass of humanity—even in our highest civilizations—is wonderfully influenced, and its actions largely controlled, by established customs and practices of the times.

When we remember that *Man* is the only animal

that nature has so elevated as to endow with even an imperfect sense of justice and mercy, we should no longer marvel at the atrocities of past generations. Conversely we should be thankful that we now have a clearer perception of things, a more accurate sense of justice; all of which carries with it an increased burden of responsibility and a greater obligation to our fellow-beings. We should be comforted concerning our misdeeds of the past by the fact that we Americans—along with most other highly civilized peoples—have attained to a moral plane which no longer tolerates slavery in any form, however greatly we may be tempted by cupidity, and the longings of the soul for pleasurable leisure at the expense of others. Those freest in the use of violent terms of expression in opposition to slavery are the immediate descendants of the very people most active in the capture and importation of Negroes to this country. They burdened the South with the frightful scourge for pecuniary gain and later demanded relinquishment of the property thus conveyed for gold. However we do not blame the one side more than the other, we all fell into the "Slough of Despond" together, but the South, being the weaker, came out naked save for its yoke of perpetual pensions to the victors—the North having relieved it of its clothing and its burden of gold and substituted for them the pension parasite, as an antidote to a reversion to its former corpulency. But this is not the proper place to discuss this feature of the subject.

The earliest transportation of African Negroes from the Old World to the New—in any considerable numbers—was that carried on by the Spanish. These savages were captured on the west coast of Africa and sold, at great profit, to early white settlers in the West Indies. Then came the Dutch, who first sent their human laden ships to the West Indies and later engaged in the trade with the British and French colonists of North America.

The circumstances of the sending of the first cargo of Negroes to that part of America, which was later to become the United States, are both interesting and instructive. We do not know the exact day, but we learn from extant record that it was on a hot day near the end of August, 1619, that the first African Negroes were landed at Jamestown, on the James river and within the boundary of what was later to form the present state of Virginia. We infer from statements contained in various extant documents that it was in the heat of the day—probably between twelve and two o'clock—that the cry went up from some of the men of the little camp known as Jamestown, who happened to be at work in full view of the river, "A ship! a ship! thank God a ship is coming in with the tide!" It is hard to imagine the excitement and thrilling emotions which this little handful of half-starved settlers experienced, at the sound of such words as these. When long ago they stood gazing at a departing ship many of them probably wondered if ever again a similar sight would fill their souls with joy. At the first announcement of an approaching ship all eyes were fixed upon her, and many a silent prayer was offered up in thanksgiving. To this mere handful of forlorn English-speaking people there was only one cry more startling, which was, "The hostile Indians are upon us!" But as yet they knew not the flag under which the vessel sailed. Spain at this time claimed all North America and the settlers knew that she was threatening to lay waste the helpless little band of British subjects. So the emotion of the settlers was a combination of joy and fear.*

There must have been great rejoicing among the little company when the curious little craft hove nearer, and they were able to distinguish the colors of the Dutch flag; for the Dutch were friendly, and at that time the leading traders of the world.

Then, too, they saw that her cannon were not manned; they were not even cast loose for action.† The movements and occupations of the men on her decks confirmed the impression otherwise gained that trade, not war, was the real object of her visit. Thus the fears of the first settlers at Jamestown were speedily dispelled, and they forthwith entered into friendly negotiations.

When the vessel had been made fast to trees—for as yet there were no wharfs—the Captain offered for sale, among other articles of merchandise, twenty black human beings, direct from the wild forest lands

---

*If we could have observed the craft it would have appeared queer indeed, she would have impressed us as too small to be seaworthy and too short for the breadth, for she was nearly round. Her ends projected high in the air, the front, or bow was called the "forecastle," and the back, or stern, the "poop." These names were very significant—ships of that time literally carried a castle at the fore-end and another at the hinder-end.

†There is an old record giving the names of some of the Negroes landed, but the name of the vessel and that of her commander are apparently lost forever. John Rolfe, the Englishman who afterwards married the barbarian Princess, Pocahontas, was a resident of Jamestown at the time the "Dutchman" brought the Negro captives, and it is from his diary that we get the following: "A dutch man of warre that sold us twenty Negroes came to Jamestown in 1619."

Other accounts speak of this ship as a Dutch trader, while others yet call her a privateer. Therefore it is perhaps correct to regard her as a sort of combination ship, desiring trade and profit but ready for war if need be—a very common type of the time.

of the Dark Continent.*

During the same year the "Treasurer," a vessel sailing under the British flag, came to the shores of the colony bearing a burden of human freight from Africa. The "Treasurer" was supposed to be the property of the Earl of Warwick, but the notorious and rapacious scoundrel, Captain Samuel Argall—who at the time was ruler of the colony of Virginia —also owned a liberal share of the ship.†

From this time on the importation of Negro captives greatly increased—for it was an exceedingly lucrative occupation—and their status soon became almost uniformly that of unconditional slavery. This state of affairs continued throughout colonial times and was not disturbed in any material way until 1808, when laws were passed by the United States Congress prohibiting the African traffic.

However, a strong sentiment against the slave-trade and the increase of Negro population existed almost from the first, and developed and ripened as the slaves became more numerous.

For more than two centuries the conditions existing along the west coast of Africa, and aboard the slavers, constituted a veritable hell. The poor defenseless savages were torn forever from every tie that

---

*These Negroes are generally believed to have been sold into absolute slavery, but recent research shows that they were sold only into limited servitude. At that time there was no statutory recognition of absolute slavery in the American colonies. Recognition of absolute slavery in the American colonies occurred in Massachusetts in 1641, in Connecticut in 1650, in Virginia in 1661, and later in all the other colonies.

†After thorough research into the history of the times it seems well within the bounds of possibility that the Treasurer—which is known to have visited the colonies during the same year —may actually have preceded the Dutchman, and thus be entitled to the odious distinction of having landed the first indentured Negroes. There is no way of definitely deciding the point.

binds, without mercy and, apparently, without shame, either to die of ill treatment or to spend the remainder of life as chattels of a superior but mercenary race, in a strange land and for the most part under the lash of hard taskmasters. When once captured they were literally without hope, and without reward. Many of them committed suicide aboard ship. Close watch had to be kept to prevent serious financial losses to the captors by this means. To think of these poor wretches being taken by cunning, deception, and sheer force, from their tribal and family relations, and placed immediately and forever under conditions of torture, is grewsome beyond expression.

As a means of economizing space they were frequently packed spoon-fashion (that is laid upon their sides so that their knees and other parts of the body fitted into each other) on a deck constructed for the purpose. In many instances they were put into irons and tied down to a hard plank floor on an ill-ventilated and poorly, if at all, lighted deck, so close to the next above that if they chanced to have a free hand it could easily be extended to the ceiling. In this position they remained during the passage— a period of from six to eight weeks. During these passages it was not uncommon for the poor creatures to die of thirst. It was until very recently a common occurrence for a ship to run short of water and on such occasions the imprisoned captives were, of course, the first to suffer. The horrors of the "middle passage," as it is called, are absolutely indescribable. In many cases—if the reader will excuse the inelegant language—these Negroes may truthfully be said to have been bound down to the filthy floor of a veritable dungeon to rot alive. The loss of a third in transit, from deprivation and its incidental diseases, was not at all unusual and it frequently happened that more than half perished before reaching their destination. The dreadful facts in these cases were concealed as far as possible, however, the evidence is preserved that in one instance, at least, the ship's crew became so depleted from death and illness—consequent upon the decaying human bodies lashed to the decks below them—that the ship came near being lost in a calm sea for want of sailors to man her.

From 1695 onward, statutes were passed imposing duties with the avowed intention of discouraging the traffic, but on account of the great margin of profit these measures all proved, alike, ineffectual. In fact it may well be doubted if those in authority ever intended to arrest the trade by the passage of such laws. It was a convenient means of replenishing the treasury and, superficially, such acts bore the garb of attempted justice. They were designed rather to appease those who feared the consequences of further increase in Negro population on the one hand, and, on the other, that much larger class who, having no interest in the profits, were clamorous for justice. The penalties were not sufficient to arrest the trade even if they had been rigidly enforced, and if we may judge from the constant and open violations their enforcement was never intended. In other words, the arrest of the abominable practice was contrary to the wishes of those in authority, which is the best of evidence that the powers behind the representatives were in reality opposed to closing our ports to the trade.

In 1818 certain members of Congress made another attempt—apparently in good faith—to enact an efficient law, but when the measure reached the President it had been so completely emasculated by members dominated through interests favorable to a continuation of Negro importations, that it was scarcely worth the paper upon which it was written. In practice it proved wholly inefficient.

At the following sessions (1819) those fearing the continuation of the trade, and the alarming increase in Negro population, succeeded in passing an act, which, if it could have been rigidly enforced would have practically ended the shameful capture and barter of these human beings. But its execution proved largely a failure, partly owing to the impossibility of guarding our entire Atlantic coast and partly in consequence of the neutrality, or open sympathy, of a large class with those engaged in the trade.

Beginning with the seventeenth century and continuing well into the nineteenth—a span of more than two hundred years—all the maritime powers of Europe, aided by the American colonies themselves, took an active part in Negro slave-trade.

Spite of the conviction and desire of a certain portion of humanity, that right should rank gain, it is lamentably true that when put to the trying test of a personal application, a distressingly large portion of the race has always been found on the side of private gain. Even in the midst of our vaunted Anglo-Saxon and Anglo-American civilizations, and in this year of our Lord 1913, this statement still holds good. In all the dark chapters of human history there are none more humiliating and shameful than the damnable annals of this Negro slave-trade. It must ever remain as an uneradicable blot on the pages of American history.

If we were under no other obligations to our black brothers, we could never free ourselves of the debt which these revolting facts entail. When we reflect upon these dark records of the deeds of our ancestors, those of us who accept the doctrine of a universal and uninterrupted reign of natural law apparently possess a more comfortable faith than those who believe in an interposing Providence; for science teaches that natural law has ordained that one living creature should ever prey upon another, and that the stronger should subjugate, and often exterminate, the weaker. In the human species we see no exception, save in so far as civilization has developed his mental faculties, thereby softening his baser animal instincts, and supplementing the simpler laws of nature.

The mother country—as we have always fondly regarded old England—deserves the highest praise for her humane attitude and action on this question of legalized capture and enslavement of human beings, during the latter years of the practice. By an act of the British parliament in the year 1833—effective August 1, 1834—twenty million pounds sterling was appropriated to provide liberty for an inferior and alien race. In addition to this (and beginning with this period) she spent annually more than five million pounds sterling and sacrificed thousands of her seamen in the maintenance of her African squadrons—all for the benefit of the despised Negro race.

On August 1, 1834, slavery for life was forever abolished within the bounds of the British Empire. This recognition of Great Britain of the obligation due an inferior and subject race by a superior and dominant one, has no parallel in history. Our own emancipation of four million slaves by a single edict is not a parallel, it being an unintentional and unforeseen consequence of civil war. Other nations have abrogated the practice of slavery, but this has usually come to pass reluctantly, and by force of circumstances,—as in our own case—in conformity to some definite internal pressure, or by reason of less definable international circumstances. In our own legislative enactments on this subject (1818-1819), members of Congress were not—as some wrongly suppose—actuated by self-sacrificing conviction of duty to an abused and weaker race; but contrariwise, their acts were scarcely less selfish than the practices of the smugglers who almost openly violated them. For the more northernly states of the Union had already found slavery unprofitable, and in the Southern states—where the institution was believed to be profitable, and planters of the great staples of cotton and tobacco constantly demanded accessions to their supply of slave labor—the more thoughtful element saw plainly the disadvantages and dangers of the ever increasing Negro population. However, most of those directly—though temporarily—benefited by human chattelism were quite willing to close their eyes and ears to existing conditions and future consequences.

CHAPTER VII

The Attitude of Christianity Toward Slavery in Colonial Times—Other Facts

MANY have made the claim that the secret of our modern civilizations, with their greatly improved moral standards, is to be sought and found in the Christian religion. If this statement is rigidly restricted to the moral teachings of Jesus it certainly contains an element of truth, but if it be made to cover the history of the church, and the practices of those calling themselves Christians, its claims will not stand the test of investigation. For the history of the church is closely associated with a most abhorrent reign of crime and bloodshed.

Christians have always condemned the cruel practices of the Mohammedans while extolling their own institutions, and teaching doctrines which they rarely practice in daily conduct. They strive to forget their own history and to conceal the records of their dark deeds from each succeeding generation. But with all their temporal authority, and wholesale murder, in past centuries, of those who loved truth even better than life, they have not been able to blot out the secular records of such inhuman conduct as the seven, or—to include only the more notorious—the four scourges of the Christian Crusaders against a people and a faith quite as sincere, if not so well founded in its initial moral precepts.

There are few if any chapters in human history more revolting, and blood-curdling, than those of the Christians against the Saracens, in the Spanish Inquisition, and the persecutions of such men as Bruno and Galileo, for teaching the great truths of nature. They conveniently forget to remember their own atrocities, while retaining a vivid recollection of the less horrifying crimes of other religions. They are more than willing to magnify and exhibit the mote in the eye of other faiths were they not blinded by the real magnitude of the beam in their own.

Let us take for instance the siege of Jerusalem and the crimes enacted within its walls on the 15th of July, 1099. After laying siege to the city for more than a month, and causing the wholesale death of men, women, and children by starvation, it was taken by storm. When finally these merciless Christians entered the city's walls they vented their wrath by indiscriminate murder. The brains of babes were beaten out against the curbstones. They spared not youth, nor age, nor sex, but murdered the poor helpless children and babies along with all conditions of men and women. Nor can they justly claim that they temporarily lost self-control in the heat of passion; for their leaders afterwards wrote home exultingly, "In Solomon's Porch and in his Temple our men rode in the blood of the Saracens up to the knees of their horses."

These highly immoral practices of so-called Christians are cited merely to show that the part played by professing Christians in our American slave-trade, as well as throughout the entire history of Negro slavery in America, is nothing strange or new. It has always been the case that Christian institutions have manifested more of *emotional profession* than of *moral example*. The more recent conduct of the various Christian'*isms*, or sects, in connection with Negro slavery, is not one whit less censurable than the crimes of the Crusaders, or the cruel practices of the Spanish Inquisition.

We have referred briefly to the merciless raids of Christian peoples upon the homes of African Negroes, during which they murdered the babes and the aged, preserving only the lives of those most salable.

It was a Christian people—or several Christian peoples—that perpetrated these intensely immoral acts. The very people who came to this country for religious freedom immediately denied the same to others. They denied the Negro the right to live, unless his existence could be readily converted into dollars and cents. We cannot cease to wonder whether or not these early Christian settlers—in their greed for gain—ever paused to reflect *what Jesus would have done* in the premises. The pessimist often tells us that humanity is growing worse; but on the whole we cannot agree with him, for there is an abundance of evidence to the contrary. But during those centuries of Negro slave-trade, and slave-holding, we Caucasians certainly lapsed into a state of mind sufficiently immoral and inhuman to have paralleled the records of any legalized practices of the past. Not one of the early colonial communities is exempt from this odium. It is true, however, that New England saw the error first, and ever after waged an honorable war against the continuation of the institution. Contrary to the general conviction of the Southern people, yet without intended reflection, it must be admitted, that (with certain prominent exceptions) the Northern half of our common country has always been—and still is—entitled to the honor of leadership in both thought and action. This is by no means a pleasant admission for a Southern man to make, but we hold it nobler to confess the truth than to appear more loyal by attempting to pervert or suppress the evidence.

Many Southern people believed that the only difference in the attitude of the two sections regarding
human chattelism was that the North found it unprofitable while the agricultural requirements of the
South made the system highly remunerative. Unquestionably this view contains a certain amount of
truth, but it has been greatly exaggerated by some
Southern people, who evinced to the bitter end, a
dogged determination to perpetuate slavery, right or
wrong, simply because it could be turned to profit—
as they thought. Like all other peoples, in all historic times, they tried to convince themselves by ingenious arguments that the course they elected to per-
sue was the moral one. As an extenuating circumstance in the South's attitude toward slavery, and the
slave-trade, it should be remembered that the Negro
is certainly a much lower order of being than the
white man, and that harsh treatment does not produce in him the mental anguish that it does in the
higher race. This, however, by no means justifies
the conclusion that he is wholly devoid of such attributes as love, sympathy, and altruism in general.
These qualities are superficially quite as intense as
in the higher races, but not perhaps so deep-seated
and enduring. Individuals have often shown themselves to be the equals of the whites in such qualities.
Mulattoes, with a preponderance of white blood,
must have been nearly equal to the master class in
these respects.

In the year 1618 (1620 some give it) when the
Dutch vessel landed the first Negro slaves at Jamestown, England and other European countries had
already largely come to look upon the practice as
contrary to justice and natural right. It was established opinion throughout Western Europe that

Christians could not be held as slaves. This immunity, however, did not extend to "infidels and heathen"—as they were wont to call all non-Christians. While all the newly established American colonies were intensely pious—in external form at least—and all held devoutly to Christianity—under one 'ism or another—they were nevertheless guilty of the absurd practice of separating their religion from, or—if you please—conforming it to the ungodly and inhuman institution of hereditary slavery. They often withheld Christianity from both slaves and free Negroes alike; the one privilege which they esteemed for themselves above all others; the one thing which "The Book" most emphatically commands them to make known to all creatures.

The reasons for this are not far to see. In the first place it seemed to them more consistent to hold pagans or infidels (as they were pleased to call those of other faiths) than Christians themselves. But a more vital reason for this is to be found in the fact that English law—the real fundamental law of the colonists—declared a Christian to be a freeman, and expressly forbade his reduction to unlimited servitude even for crime.

One of the chief sources of attempts to justify slavery is to be found in the antiquated, so-called, moral teachings of Moses.

In the colony of Massachusetts, and in the year 1641, a body of what they called fundamental laws was promulgated—in more modern usage we would say, a constitution was adopted, for this was to serve them as their organic law as long as the King did not interfere and its contents were not found to be inconsistent with English law. One of these articles, based on the Mosaic code, provides that "There shall never be any bond slavery, villeinage, nor captivity among us, unless it be lawful captives, taken in just wars, and such strangers as willingly sell themselves or are sold unto us, and these shall have all the liberties and Christian usages which the law of God established in Israel requires" (which are none). "This exempts none from servitude who shall be judged thereunto by authority."

This law refers to the "Christian usages established in Israel." Now this could not have been an oversight, for Moses did not teach the Israelites Christianity, or Christian usages, since he lived thousands of years before the time of Jesus. Moreover, his followers rejected Christianity at the time of its inauguration, and have steadfastly remained in opposition to it.

Some may interpret this Massachusetts act as indicating an undue regard for the antiquated Jewish law, but more correctly it is a shrewd process of "whipping the devil around the stump" to meet their selfish ends. The declared intention of this colonial Constitution to conform strictly to "the law of God established in Israel" appealed strongly to a certain truly pious element in the community. Not that the law meant anything—for its real purport was the exact opposite from the construction put upon it—but simply because the phraseology was pious. In that community, as in others, and then as at present, a certain class sincerely believed and strenuously contended that established religious dogma should forever rank reason and progress. The absurdity of such a position may be illustrated by the following quotation from the fourteenth chapter of Deuteronomy and the twenty-first verse: "Ye shall not eat of anything that dieth of itself; thou shalt give it unto the stranger that is in thy gates, that he may eat it; or thou mayest sell it unto an alien." No people can follow such doctrine as this and hope to advance to higher moral ideals.

We take it that when Dr. Charles Wm. Eliot, of Harvard, said we needed a new religion he had in mind, not—as some would pervert his words to mean—a remodeling of our moral code downward, but that the people needed a purer, more modern, and higher code of moral precept and practice.

If at the time of the planting of the colonies of Jamestown and Plymouth we could have produced a new Moses to have given us a new moral code, based on pure living, and teaching the people to be good and just, to regard altruism always above egoism, because it is right so to live, and because human experience has proven that high and unselfish living is the only road to the fullest attainment of personal happiness, we would never have had a Negro problem. Such a code would have shown the injustice of human chattelism, and saved us the penalties of violated natural rights, which we have suffered ever since. We reluctantly abandoned the practice of slavery, but as yet have not been able to shake off its shackels.

The last sentence of the quotation from the Massachusetts Constitution—"This exempts none from servitude who shall be judged thereunto by authority"—was evidently added to make sure that the laws of the ancient Israelites could not be misconstrued, so as to admit of interference, in any way, with the practice of absolute slavery of Negroes. This article not only permitted slavery and the Negro slave-trade, but it also enabled the colonists to capture, buy, sell, and use as they pleased, the American Indians, who were unable to protect themselves against their superior enemies who had already taken from them the territory itself.

Just in proportion as Man has increased in wisdom he has advanced in moral standards, and this may be applied alike to nations and individuals; for the former is really but a reflection of the latter. But, in a large measure, it is unfortunately true that *"might" rather than "right" prevails.* We have advanced and improved wonderfully in moral standards since the early settlement of this country. No better evidence of this is needed than the fact that the cruel practices of slavery in any form have been abandoned.

Occasionally we still hear it contended that the War of Secession, or of the Rebellion—as you please—was waged largely through prejudice and jealousy on the part of the Northern states, however, such was not the case. But, no doubt, there existed a class of New Englanders who were more or less biased and bitter toward their sister states of the South, and likewise a corresponding class of Southerners who detested the North.

Underlying all this there was a profound and growing conviction that slavery was unjust, immoral, and dangerous to the people and the nation.

In colonial times, or during that portion of our history antedating the revolt against the mother country slavery in proportion to its numbers, involved far more human suffering than in its later stages. The Negroes who were torn from their native heaths and forever separated from family ties, and all else dear to them, suffered far more than those born in America who—in some instances at least—were allowed to live among their relations and friends. Up to the very end of slavery there were importations from Africa, but more latterly the vast majority of slaves were native born Afro-Americans.

With these early slaves, in fact with all Negro American slaves, the chance for improvement was slight; they were generally denied book-learning even for religious purposes. But they could not be denied the opportunity to observe the conduct and works of their masters, which in itself had the effect of civilizing and improving the Negro character. In order to give the reader a clearer outline of the real hardships of slavery in colonial times, and to support our own statements of the facts by extant records, we will quote in the following chapter certain extracts from laws bearing on the subject.

CHAPTER VIII

Harsh Laws and Regulations of Negro Slaves in Colonial Times

FROM the planting of the colony of Virginia at Jamestown, and that of Massachusetts, at Plymouth, until long after the War of Revolution, and the independence of the thirteen original colonies, Virginia was an undisputed leader among her sister commonwealths. She supplied more statesmen and more great soldiers than any other colony or state. She also took first rank in formulating laws and regulations suited to the new conditions.

Thus we find that the "Old Dominion"—as she was later familiarly and affectionately called—enacted more laws concerning the Negro slave-trade, and the regulation of slaves, than any other state. At least this appears to be true from such documentary evidence as has been preserved. Possibly it is only *apparent,* because of the high regard of the other colonies for the acts of the early House of Burgesses, and later legislation by Virginia's General Assembly. Certain it is that the other colonies looked up to her as a kind of mother and leader in this Negro question, as in all others.

Up to the year 1662 the white settlers in the colony of Virginia were virtually a law unto themselves as regards their Negro chattels, for they had no statutory laws on the subject and English law of the day prescribed that no Christian could be held as a slave, and English courts discouraged, in every pos-

III

sible way, a system so obviously contrary to natural rights.

At the time of the settlement of Jamestown slavery was rapidly disappearing in England by individual emancipation. However there was no English law expressly forbidding slavery of non-Christians in the colonies.

We may easily imagine the rough treatment that the early black people received in this and other settlements, for the white emigrants were not all English gentlemen, nor were they all religious enthusiasts, as some seem to suppose. But even if they had been—as we have said elsewhere—the customs of the times combined with the well-nigh universal human failing of selfish greed would have afforded the poor devils scant mercy.

The imported African savages and their descendants virtually had no rights in any of the early colonies; the master was free to do with them as he pleased; he could force them to work, chastise them, use them for the gratification of his animal passions, and even murder them, at his own individual choice and caprice. They were in the truest sense chattels, and, for the most part, so remained to the end of slavery. Under such freedom of action on the part of the masters, their treatment was very bad. There were, of course, in Virginia, as elsewhere, certain noble men and women who made the condition of their slaves ideal;—so far as the term can be applied to an immoral practice—and in many instances they were greatly humored and spoiled; but this was the rare exception, and even in these instances it more frequently applied only to certain favorite house-servants, and not to the far more numerous class of men and women who tilled the soil under taskmasters and overseers—field-hands as they were called.

The first acts of the Virginia legislature to define and regulate slavery were not for the betterment of the condition of these humble people; they perhaps made their treatment more cruel and inhuman. We get our best views of the attitude of the dominant class towards their human chattels from the general tenor of these early laws.

It was at a session of the Virginia legislature in December, 1662, that the first attempt was made to give a legislative basis to the system of hereditary slavery. It was enacted that children should be held bond or free "according to the condition of the mother." Under this act it not infrequently happened that a master's illegitimate children were foreordained to the life and horrors of absolute slavery under their own father.

Virginia's next legislative enactment on the subject was in 1667. It provided that Negroes, though converted and baptised into Christianity, should not thereby become free. This was in direct opposition to English law, which declared that no Christian could be held as a slave; but the mother country showed no inclination to interfere.

At the same session it was also enacted that killing slaves by extremity of correction should not be esteemed felony, "since it cannot be presumed that prepense malice should induce any man to destroy his own estate." This unjust act was also contrary to English law.

Since there were some good people who freed their slaves from time to time, the Virginia legislature now passed an act subjecting freed Negroes to complete civil disabilities.

Again in 1682 the code of Virginia—regarding slavery—was augmented by the following additions: Slaves were denied the right to carry arms, either offensive or defensive, or to go off the plantation of their masters without a written pass, or to lift hand against a Christian even in self-defense. Runaways refusing to be apprehended might be lawfully killed.

In 1692 Virginia passed an act entitled "An act for suppressing outlying slaves," after setting forth in a preamble that "Many times Negroes, mulattoes, and other slaves unlawfully absent themselves from their masters' and mistresses' service, and lie hid, and lurk in obscure places, killing hogs, and committing other injuries to the inhabitants of the dominion," authorizes any two justices—one constituting a quorum—to issue their warrants to the sheriff for the arrest of any such outlying slaves. Whereupon the sheriff is to use the necessary force, and if such slaves resist, or run away, or refuse to surrender, they may be lawfully killed and destroyed "by guns, or any other way whatsoever," the master, in such cases, to receive from the public four thousand pounds of tobacco for the loss of his slave.*

It was not an unusual occurrence in Virginia for a poor, misused Negro, or mulatto—sometimes virtually white—to be driven to desperation and attempt to live the life of a recluse and marauder. This was more common perhaps among those slaves who were more than half white.

The author is himself a native Virginian and can testify of his own knowledge to the fact that some of these very light colored mulattoes, who for the most part have only such cultivation as they have acquired unaided, are men of magnificent Caucasic mental endowment. Under such circumstances it is

---

*Clauses included in quotation marks are the exact wording of extracts from the laws—much of the rest is taken directly from these laws but the exact language is not always closely followed.

easy to understand that his lot as a chattel was often beyond his power of endurance. Such men would sometimes conclude that they would rather take a long chance at eking out an existence as wild men in the forests, than be kicked and cuffed about by their masters, who were often their very nearest of blood relations, or, in many instances, human brutes, who violated every law of humanity in their treatment of Negro slaves. Here is a special act made to fit such a case:

About the year 1700 we find a Virginia act setting forth that "One Billy, a Negro slave to John Tittel, has several years unlawfully absented himself from his master's service, lying out, and lurking in obscure places, supposedly within the counties of James City, York, and Kent, devouring and destroying the stocks and crops, robbing the homes of, and committing and threatening other injuries to several of his majesty's good and liege people within this colony and dominion of Virginia, in contempt of the good laws thereof;" wherefore the said Billy is declared by the act guilty of a capital offense; and, "whosoever shall kill and destroy the said Negro slave Billy, and apprehend and deliver him to justice," is to be rewarded with a thousand pounds of tobacco; and of persons entertaining him, or trading and trucking with him, are declared guilty of felony; his master, if he be killed, to receive a compensation from the public of four thousand pounds of tobacco."

It is clearly discernible, from a careful consideration of these early statutes, that the whole social status of the times was so far removed from present conditions that it is difficult for us to imagine it. For instance, it was found necessary, as we shall presently show, to pass specific acts and impose penalties upon white women for having Negro children.

This fact alone should have great weight in convincing the pessimist and advocate of amalgamation that we are not only becoming more moral, but that the possibility of amalgamation is further from us to-day than at any period in the history of the country. Our observation leads us, in fact, to the conclusion that no imaginable change in existing social conditions would prove potent in bringing to pass such an abomination to any considerable extent.

The real truth is,—paradoxical though it may seem,—the population of our day is less *religious* and far more *moral,* in every way than were our colonial ancestors. Take for instance the intermarriage of white women with Negro men and illegitimate childbearing of white women by cohabitation with Negro men; a common occurrence in colonial times, which had to be carefully restricted by laws—but almost unknown at present.

It is true Virginia has a law in force to-day which prohibits such marriages in either direction; but we have rarely known of a white woman giving birth to an illegitimate mulatto child.

With thirty times the population she had in 1700 we doubt, if every birth could be carefully investigated, if a single such instance would be recorded in a twelve months. The Virginia statute which we last cited, for the suppression or murder of outlying Negro slaves, also contains the following: "For the prevention of that abominable mixture and spurious issue which hereafter may increase in this dominion, as well by Negroes, mulattoes, and Indians intermarrying with English or other white women, as by their unlawful accompanying with one another, any free white man or woman intermarrying with a Negro, mulatto or Indian, is to be forever banished.'" A few years later this punishment was changed to six months' imprisonment and a fine of ten pounds sterling. White women having mulatto children without marriage were to pay fifteen pounds sterling, or be sold for five years; that period, if they were servants, to take effect from the expiration of their former term, the mulatto children thus born were to be bound out as servants (term-slavery) until they were thirty years old.

Still another feature of this same act attempted to discourage the emancipation of Negroes. It provided that no Negro or mulatto slave should be set free, unless the emancipator paid for his transportation out of the country within six months. This act did not render void the manumission, but only subjected the emancipator who violated it to a fine of ten pounds. It further provided that the fine thus imposed should be applied or appropriated towards the transportation of the freed slave out of the colony.

Another remarkable deviation from the English law was an act put in force about this time for special summary tribunals, for the trial of slaves charged with crimes. Any slave judged guilty of any offense punishable by the law of England with death or loss of members, was to be forthwith committed to the county jail, there to be kept "well laden with irons," and upon notice of the fact, the governor was to issue a commission to any person of the county he might see fit, before whom the prisoner was to be arraigned, indicted, and tried, "without the solemnity of a jury," and on oath of two witnesses, or one witness, "with pregnant circumstances," or confession, was to be found guilty and sentenced.

This virtually meant that the poor devil had no legal protection at all, but was completely at the mercy of whomever chanced to be his master or judge; who, in this case was as likely to be a conscienceless slave-trader, or a merciless brute, as an honorable gentleman.

This same law also provides that the owner should be strictly accountable and responsible for damages done "by any Negro or other slave living at a quarter where there is no Christian overseer."

A fifth revision of the Virginia code was made by a committee from the council of Burgesses. Its work was in progress during the space of five years from 1700 to 1705. This new code provides that "all servants imported or brought into this country by sea or land, who were not Christians in their native country, (except Turks and Moors in amity with his Majesty, and others who can make due proof of their being free in England or any other Christian country before they were shipped in order to transportation thither,) shall be accounted, and be slaves, notwithstanding a conversion to Christianity afterwards," although they may have been born in England; "all children to be bond or free, according to the condition of their mother."

This fifth revised code cited above also contained the first provision which could be construed to take into consideration the well-being or happiness of Negro slaves and this seems to have been brought about, not by the masters taking thought for the domestic felicity and stability of the despised Negroes, but as a means of protection of the land and slave-holder against his just debtors. By a provision of this code slaves were made real estate and thus became more or less permanent fixtures. The slaves, however, did not, by this act, become wholly free from seizure for debt; in fact, they remained liable as before, but provision was made by which the heir of the plantation could buy out the inherited interests of others in the Negroes who dwelt upon it. This feature continued in force to the end of British control.

For the benefit of those not familiar with the system of government under which the early colonists lived, it may be well to state that all legislative acts by the colonists had to be submitted to his majesty the King, by the governor of the colony, who was an appointee of the King. Articles thus submitted were either approved or rejected. It was a standing instruction of the King to the governor, not to consent to the re-enactment of any law once rejected by the King, without express leave first obtained upon representation of the reasons and necessities for it.

In 1751 Virginia revised and consolidated all the laws which we have referred to into one act "concerning servants and slaves." This act embodied all the horrors and cruelties contained in those already given; some of the strictures being slightly modified. The strange feature is that the King revoked this consolidated Negro slave law, and while it does not appear that his consent was afterwards given, it was re-enacted within a year and continued in force to the end of his Majesty's authority by the War of Revolution.*

Similar laws were enacted in other colonies. For instance, we find records of the introduction of slaves into New Amsterdam (New York) about the year 1650, and the first Dutch laws concerning them were the most favorable anywhere recorded during the

---

*It is worthy of note that at the close of the Revolution the Negro population (Negro and mulatto) constituted not less than a sixth part of the total population of the United States; which is a much larger percentage of black population than we have today.

whole history of Negro slavery in America. Most of them remained the property of the Dutch Company, and the more trusty and industrious—after a limited servitude—were granted small farms, paying on an equitable and easy plan a certain amount of produce. This treatment by the Dutch sounds more like the conduct of a people with souls and human sympathies than anything to be found on the subject of slavery in the entire records of colonial history. However strange and inconsistent it may appear this emancipation did not extend to Negro children. The Dutch commonalty of the day declared it to be extraordinary and incomprehensible to them, that children, born of a free Christian mother, could nevertheless be slaves.

In a code of laws known as the "Duke's Laws," enacted for the government of New York in 1665, there is a provision that "no Christian shall be kept in bond slavery, villeinage, or captivity, except such as shall be judged thereunto by authority, or such as willingly have sold or shall sell themselves," in which case a record of such servitude shall be entered in the court of sessions "held for that jurisdiction where the master shall inhabit." This provision was evidently intended to meet the demands of Christians who felt that common decency required some law that at least *appeared* to afford the unfortunate black man some measure of protection and justice. But it did not exempt the non-Christian Negroes from any sort of ill-usage, and the words, "except such as shall be judged thereunto by authority" practically rendered the whole act null and void.*

It seems to have been even more common in early

---

*This act is almost identical in its wording with an early Massachusetts act elsewhere given.

colonial times than at present to place such meaningless laws on the statute books in response to public
demands, or demands from some influential class.
The following is a good illustration of a meaningless
or dead-letter law of our own times:

Very recently in Virginia an organized demand
was made upon a legislative assembly, by certain
leading theologians in the name of their pious following, for the passage of an act prohibiting the
hauling of freight by public carriers on Sunday. The
various members of the legislature, and particularly
the leaders, saw that they were between the devil
and the blue sea. Some plan had to be devised that
would meet the demands of the churches in order to
hold the votes of their members in future elections;
on the other hand they were confronted with the
same political necessities regarding the railroads, as
well as the necessity of protecting the mutual interests of the whole community; the future votes of all
interests had to be considered. What did they do?
They simply passed an act declaring in the most
positive terms that freight should not be moved on
Sunday; then they qualified this near the end of the
bill—in the fewest possible words—by saying, unless some perishable articles, such as fresh vegetables, had to be moved to prevent unreasonable
loss. This made it easy, of course, for the transportation company to put into the train one or more
cars containing perishable articles, or articles supposed to be perishable; and the trains moved almost
as freely as before, while the pious members of the
community had the satisfaction of feeling that they
had fully performed their religious duty, and the
politicians retained the support of all interests.

Just so it was with most of these early laws concerning the holding of slaves as chattels. They were

so worded as to make the impression on the community at large that they ameliorated the condition
and hardships of a servile race; while any one taking
the trouble to reflect upon their real purport, and
proper interpretation, saw at once that the master
was in almost every instance left free to use and
abuse his slaves at will.

Bearing in mind the above facts let us dissect the
extract from that portion of the early Massachusetts
law given in the preceding chapter, the first positive
enactment on the subject of Negro slavery: "There
shall never be any bond slavery, villeinage, nor captivity among us, unless it be lawful captives, taken
in just wars, and such strangers as willingly sell
themselves or are sold unto us, and these shall have
all the liberties and Christian usages which the law
of God established in Israel requires. This exempts
none from servitude who shall be judged thereunto
by authority."

The first words here quoted,—"there shall never
be any bond slavery, villeinage, nor captivity among
us,"—are calculated to create the impression that
the ruling class was a lofty-minded people, determined, not only to be moral and just, but to live up
to the highest ideals of the most godly men in their
conduct toward that portion of the race who were
unable to protect themselves. This however was
a mere subterfuge, offered as a sop to that minority,
which we always have with us, and who are resolved
to "do justly and to love mercy and to walk humbly
with their God," whether or not this course is consistent with their material interests. This class always puts right before every other consideration.
Then, also, it satisfied more completely that other
much larger class who like the Pharisees, were desir-
ous only of impressing their fellow-men with their

piety; but apart from that cared little or nothing for real justice. They, too, are still conspicuously with us. The next clause of the same sentence reads as follows: "unless it be lawful captives, taken in just wars, and such strangers as willingly sell themselves or are sold unto us." This portion of the sentence renders the first clause absolutely meaningless and sanctions slavery without any restrictions whatsoever, and without the least protection to such chattels; which those interested clearly understood were to be made hereditary slaves and articles of trade and barter.

The third clause of the same sentence is very cleverly put, and is intended to meet the demands of at least three classes, each holding its principles to be in opposition to, or inconsistent with, the others. And the astute drafter of the act has shown himself equal to the occasion. Here are the simple words: "And these shall have all the liberties and Christian usages which the law of God established in Israel requires." Now in that day and time there is no doubt that to the really moral class, of ordinary lay citizens, as well as to that much larger class, of religious pretenders, this clause of the act seemed to guarantee to the Negro slave absolute religious freedom; but to the legally trained mind it was of no such purport; it might as well have been left unsaid, apart from its influence upon certain citizens by virtue of the religious cloak which covered and completely nullified, what were supposed to be its more vital parts. Let us examine the clause more carefully: It tells us in substance that slaves shall have all the liberties and Christian usages which the law of God established in Israel requires. Now the old Jewish law which is implicit in the Pentateuch, (the first five books of the old testament) is not a law

of religious liberty, but a law of the strictest civil
and religious compulsion. For as we have observed
in substance, in the preceding chapter it contained
neither Christian liberties nor Christian usages; for
this people (the Israelites) later expressly denied
the claims of the Nazarene to divinity. They have
always been diametrically opposed to Christianity.
Not that they denied the wisdom of much that Jesus
is said to have taught, but that they disbelieved and
resented his claims to divinity. These facts in themselves cause that feature of this early Massachusetts
law, to expressly, and purposely, appear to be what
it is not; for Israel knew not Christianity in any of
the multifarious forms which it was to assume in
centuries yet unborn.

Moreover, if this leaves the clause with any apparent meaning whatsoever it can be none other
than such moral tenets as are contained in the Pentateuch. What then do we find in the clause to comfort the despised and ill-treated Negro slave? Of
all the bigoted and selfish peoples the world has ever
known these ancient Israelites are perhaps the most
conspicuous example. They taught and believed that
they were a chosen people of God and that it was
pious, honorable, and commendable for a Hebrew
to outwit and impose upon any and all other races
of mankind.

A law, therefore, purporting to have been enacted
for the benefit and protection of an inferior, down-
trodden, and enslaved people, based upon a set of
writings so obviously constructed for the benefit of a
superior race at the expense of all others, cannot
properly be regarded as anything but a subterfuge,
intended to impress, appease and deceive certain
classes of clamorous citizens. One of these classes
really demanded justice; another, cared only for os-

tentatious display of piety; while a third—who really enacted the law—took particular pains to make sure that its provisions had no serious bearing on the *status quo*.

The concluding sentence of this Massachusetts enactment, "(This exempts none from servitude who shall be judged thereunto by authority)" was added to make certain that even if the subtle immorality of the rest of the act, had, in every case, been otherwise construed, this closing sentence would completely nullify the godly-sounding words that preceded it. The direct quotations which we have given are sufficient to supply the reader with a clear perception of the general tenor and purport of these early laws, as well as to show the conditions under which the black race lived from the settlement of the colonies to the revolt against England.

As to the attitude of the several sections there seems to have been no well-defined differences in their treatment of the slave question, except as regards the Dutch settlement of New Amsterdam (New York), which was much more liberal and considerate than the rest. The later differences and prejudices between North and South appear to have been necessary evil consequences of national development. As the nation evolved, sectional and local interests diverged and prejudices developed, until at last, with the heat of passion centred around the great question of human slavery, the glowing coals burst into flame, and the devastating scourge of War of Secession was upon us.

This early slave-trade and the legislative acts for its regulation are certainly deplorable chapters in our national life, and since they are past and gone forever it seems the part of wisdom to let them— along with all subsequent acts of cruelty and brutality in this connection—rest as quietly as possible, except in so far as they can be made to serve in well-meaning benevolent efforts to solve the great and threatening Negro question, which at this moment casts a very dark—but we believe a slowly dissipating—shadow over the continued peace and prosperity of this nation.

CHAPTER IX

The Status of the Negro, and Negro Slavery, During the Closing Years of British Sovereignty, and Under the Confederation

THERE is nowhere to be found a proverb more pregnant with truth than that governments are as good, and no better, than their units—the individuals who compose them; governments are, in consequence, found to vary somewhat with different peoples, and in different times, according to the individual and composite character of their citizenship. Therefore it must be admitted that, at best, human government is very imperfect and never entirely free from corruption.

Thus we find—contrary to the belief of some—that the average standard of justice and right among the early colonists was—largely through ignorance—none too high. It was distinctly lower than that of the later period, of government under the Confederation, and under the Constitution.

In accordance with the principle just stated the dreadful condition and treatment of the subject Negro race were somewhat better under the Confederation, and continued to improve, slowly, under the Constitution, until we reached a point when the moral standards of the whole people had been so elevated that slavery was no longer tolerable.

It should be well remembered—as a point to be made use of in our later argument, concerning the final solution of the Negro question—that this emancipation did not come to the black race through any effort, or ability, to assert its rights; it was wholly through the improved moral standards of the greater portion of our white population. In other words the Negro possessed no ability whatsoever to help or free himself. So long as he had plenty of food and outlets for his ordinary animal passions, he remained happy and content. We could not have held as chattels that number of Jews, or even a like number of Japanese. In fact it is questionable if it would have been possible to enslave and so grossly punish and abuse a similar number of Amerinds. The modest mental capacities of the Negro were, in the first instance, the secret of his capture and reduction to unlimited servitude; and, secondly, the explanation of his peaceful submission, in great numbers, to a condition of absolute slavery extending over a period of centuries.

In the year 1776, and after, laws were passed and attempts made to abolish slavery in the colony of Massachusetts, and juries, in one case after another, uniformly declared that the laws then on the statute books did not sanction slavery. Their decisions from that time onward were invariably against slavery and in favor of freedom. This enlightened and progressive attitude of Massachusetts had contemporaneous support by the courts of England.

About this time the celebrated case of one James Sumersett was brought before the court of Kings bench in England. This suit was brought on a writ of *habeas corpus* and argued, first before Lord Mansfield, and then before the full court. The final opinion, handed down by Lord Mansfield, that there was no positive law to support slavery in England, and, therefore, the black must be discharged. This noted case seems to have established a lasting precedent and settled the question in England in favor of universal human freedom for all future time.

Notwithstanding the fact that every case brought before a jury in the commonwealth of Massachusetts after 1776, resulted in individual freedom, it failed to produce any general emancipation. This of course was due to the inherent greed of a large class of citizens. They were holding fast to this pernicious practice, regardless of its established injustice and immorality.

A year or two later a declaration inserted into the Massachusetts Bill of Rights declared that "all men are born free and equal." Taken literally this statement, which Jefferson had already incorporated into the Declaration of American Independence, is certainly far from true. However, the Supreme Court of Massachusetts held that this Declaration prohibited slavery within her confines; thus annulling all legal claims to property rights in human beings, so far as that colony or commonwealth, was concerned.

In the very recent, and excellent, publication of the late Honorable B. B. Munford of Richmond, Virginia, on "Virginia's Attitude Toward Slavery and Secession," his patriotism, and commendable ardor, to place the most favorable construction on Virginia's attitude regarding these questions, seem at times to have dominated his better judgment, and caused him—in spite of the noblest intentions—to violate certain recorded facts of history. For instance he gives Virginia credit for a position which unquestionably belongs to Massachusetts, by virtue of the latter's laws and court-decrees herein related.

Mr. Munford says: "Foremost among the laws enacted by her General Assembly after Virginia's declaration of independence from British rule was her celebrated statute prohibiting the slave-trade. This act was passed in 1778,—thus antedating by thirty years the like action of Great Britain. By this law it was provided 'that from and after the passing of this act no slaves should hereafter be imported into this commonwealth by sea or land, nor shall any slave so imported be sold or bought by any person whatsoever.' The statute imposed a fine of one thousand pounds upon the person importing them for each slave imported, and also a fine of five hundred pounds upon any person buying or selling any such slave for each slave bought or sold. The crime of bringing in slaves is still further guarded against by a provision which declares that every slave 'shall upon such importation become free.' Of this act Mr. Ballagh, in his History of Slavery in Virginia, says, 'Virginia thus had the honor of being the first political community in the civilized modern world to prohibit the pernicious traffic.' "

In thus sanctioning the comment and claim of Mr. Ballagh, Mr. Munford—like Mr. Ballagh—went a little too far, for Massachusetts, by a combination of her organic law and a decision of her highest judiciary, had two years previously (1776) struck a death-blow at the very root of the vile practice, and sounded the death-knell of human chattelism so far as her jurisdiction was concerned. Moreover, England had at or about the same time,—by the court-decree which we have given,—permanently abolished slavery.

Therefore, admitting the wisdom of the Virginia act quoted, and commending it so far as it goes, Massachusetts was and is clearly entitled to the high honor which the esteemed author so sincerely computes to Virginia. The very fact that the author himself is a son of Virginia would incline him to be the more scrupulous and painstaking in assigning historic honor and glory where such glory and honor justly belong.

The truth to tell—painful though it be—Virginia was holding fast to slavery with the most severe statutes for its regulation, on the one hand, while on the other, expressing her outraged sense of justice at the continuation of the African trade. And it does not require extraordinary powers of penetration into the motives of men to see the sinister side of such legislation as the Honorable B. B. Munford, with the best of intentions, accredited to her as righteousness.

May we ask what were her motives for this inconsistent attitude?

History tells us that at this time the number of black slaves in Virginia—as in other Southern states—was rapidly approaching the total number of free whites, and that in certain districts the former actually outnumbered the latter; that the people were greatly alarmed at the rapid increase of new captives from Africa, who under such cruel and inhuman treatment as they frequently received, could only hate their captors and entertain the strongest possible desire for revenge or escape. Furthermore, it was found less dangerous, cheaper, and in every respect more satisfactory to breed the black slave women, than to import new captives.

In these matters of history let us tell the unvarnished truth fearlessly; for there is nothing permanently to be gained by its perversion. Viewed in this true light we do not see that Virginia has any good reason to boast of the act in question.

On the other hand it may be said, with equal force, that the laws of Massachusetts and the Supreme Court decisions, which abolished legal slavery in that commonwealth, were in entire conformity with what the free whites of that political community conceived to be their highest self-interest. Massachusetts did not need or desire slave labor as did the agricultural South; and she saw that the moral and industrial effect of the institution was contrary to the highest interests and development of her free citizens; it tended to produce a sentiment among her white citizens that labor was dishonorable. The immediate cause of this sentiment was the fact that labor of any kind brought the free whites to a plane of equality—at least industrially—with Negro slaves.

Human nature is not, after all, so different as our egotism inclines us to suppose. It will generally be found, if we scrutinize with sufficient care, that legislative acts—like all other human acts—are founded primarily, either in the interests of an individual, or a collection of individuals, either composed of, or directly influencing, those entrusted with their making.

There can be no question of doubt that during the period immediately preceding the Revolution there was a rapidly developing sentiment in the New England states, against human slavery. Most of their own historians have given as a basis of such sentiment that they did not believe such chattelism right, and it is certain that such is partly the truth,—for it is hard to conceive how any right-thinking human being could conclude otherwise—but it is a much fuller statement of truth to admit that that section of the country was more strongly impelled by a conviction, that the institution militated against its material welfare.

Under the original Confederation, or during the brief interval between the calling of the second Continental Congress (in 1775) and the putting into effect of the present written Constitution—at the close of the year 1788—there was little or no change either in the status of the African slave-trade or the harsh regulations and treatment of slaves. There were wise and noble men in all the colonies who deplored slavery, and the slave-trade, and who did all they could against it by precept as well as by example; but this type of man was sadly in the minority, at least so far as the Southern states were concerned. The example of Massachusetts may be taken as a fair criterion of the attitude of New England in general, which, as we have said, now saw that the institution and practice was opposed to its future safety and material well-being.

When the National Constitutional Convention opened its sessions in Independence Hall in Philadelphia, on the 14th of May, 1787, this question of slavery, and the slave-trade, was one of the most perplexing with which its members were confronted; and while that splendid instrument—in its final draft —was essentially a compromise, its attitude towards the Negro question was nothing short of a complete straddle, where absolute evasion was found impossible. It is not hard to find the underlying causes for this course; the wonder is that they were ever able to agree upon anything, in the presence of such diversified opinions and conflicting interests. For instance, we have seen that the New England states not only had comparatively *few* slaves but they had found by experience that the institution—under the conditions then existing in that section of the country—was at once unprofitable and demoralizing; while in the cotton, rice and tobacco states of the South, the *consensus* of opinion was to the effect that inherited slavery was highly profitable and must be guaranteed and perpetuated.

Each Southern member of this Convention was required to define his position on the Negro slave question before he could be selected to serve his people in this all-important capacity. Thus when they came to confer in open session they found their views,—as well as those of their constituents—diametrically opposed in many cases. This was not all, such liberal intellects, as a majority of the members possessed, might have been expected to waive much in order to agree upon a matter of such vital importance as was the work in hand. But when they had expended their energies in framing such a compromise it was wholly inoperative and meaningless until it had been duly ratified by the Conventions of nine out of the total number of thirteen states.

The instrument, as it was at length agreed upon, is dated September 17, 1787. It was at once transmitted to Congress with the recommendation that it be submitted to the several State Conventions for ratification, which was accordingly done. It was adopted by eleven states in the following order: Delaware, December 7, 1787; Pennsylvania, December 12th; New Jersey, December 18th; Georgia, January 2, 1788; Connecticut, January 9th; Massachusetts, February 7th; Maryland, April 28th; South Carolina, May 23d; and New Hampshire, June 21st, which made the instrument effective, being the required ninth state ratifying. Virginia ratified June 27th; New York, July 26th. North Carolina and Rhode Island did not ratify the Constitution until 1789 and 1790 respectively.

The ratification of the Constitution by the states encountered its most serious opposition in Massachusetts, New York, and Virginia, where for a time its ultimate fate—so far at least as these states were concerned—was a matter of the gravest doubt. In their conventions there were men on both sides of the question of ratification, who had been members of the National Convention, associated with others of distinguished abilities. There were adverse influences in Massachusetts that would almost certainly have defeated ratification in that state, had not the proposition been accompanied by a bill of rights and proposed amendments, to be submitted by Congress to the several states for their sanction. The adoption of these by the convention gained the support of Hancock and Samuel Adams for the Constitution; and the question of ratification was carried by a vote of one hundred and eighty-seven to one hundred and sixty-eight.

We moderns seem to think a great deal more of the Constitution than did the leading men who controlled the nation and steered the ship of state at the time that organic law was made the most influential writing of the age, and destined to become later the guiding star of the greatest temporal power in history.

This instrument was vehemently opposed in the Virginia Convention by such brilliant lights and world-renowed statesmen as James Monroe, George Mason, and Patrick Henry—Mason having also been a member of the famous Convention that framed it. Arrayed on the other side were such men as Mr. Madison, Mr. Pendleton, John Marshall, Edmond Randolph and George Wythe; three of whom were also members of the National Convention of framers. Mr. Randolph, who had refused to sign the instrument, had become one of its strongest advocates. Here again we find the ratification advocates greatly aided by a bill of rights and certain proposed amendments. It is quite certain that the Constitution could never have been ratified by the required number of states had it not been for the promise of certain amendments and the adoption of bills of rights. Under the circumstances the organic law of this great republic was finally ratified by the Virginia legislature by a vote of eighty-eight yeas against eighty nays.

In New York the opposition was even stronger than in Virginia, and ratification was made possible in the final vote, of thirty-one to twenty-nine, only by the previous adoption of a bill of rights and numerous amendments; and in the National Convention of framers two of New York's three delegates actually went so far as to withdraw. Among the opponents were Yates, Lansing, and George Clinton; the two former being members also of the General Convention; while its strongest advocates were John Jay, Robert R. Livingston, and Mr. Hamilton.

All of the states were very tardy about ratification and some appear to have waited to see what their sister states would do.

The injunction of secrecy as to the proceedings of the National Convention was never removed. In accordance with a previous vote the Journal was entrusted to the custody of Washington, by whom it was afterward deposited in the department of state, and by order of Congress it was first printed in 1818. Yates,—one of the members from New York,—took short notes of the earlier debates, which were published after his death in 1821. The more perfect notes of Madison, published later with the official Journal, the notes of Yates, and a representation to the legislature of Maryland made by Luther Martin, furnished materials for a more or less complete view of the conflicting opinions which divided the convention, and of a process of attrition and compromise over matters of the most vital interest, which finally molded the Federal Constitution out of the original mass of once chaotic views. For few if any of the men that constituted the convention were themselves satisfied with the composite structure which, in the end, represented no individual perfectly, but was perhaps the best that could be done, and no doubt much better than any individual member could have produced.

We have said that the instrument was a straddle on the vital question of Negro slavery. How could it have been otherwise when half the men in the Convention believed it to be unjust to the Negro, and injurious, or ruinous, to the morality and industry of the whites; while the other half looked upon the black man as a legitimate chattel, and his condition as essential to the prosperity of the Southern half of the country?

In the following extracts from articles of the Constitution we give the only portions which are supposed to relate even vaguely to the question of slavery.

Preamble. "We the people of the United States, in order to form a more perfect Union, establish justice, insure domestic tranquility for the common defense, promote the general welfare and secure the blessings of liberty to ourselves and our posterity, do ordain this Constitution for the United States of America.

Article I. Section 1. "All legislative powers herein granted, shall be vested in a Congress of the United States, which shall consist of a Senate and a House of Representatives.

Section 2. "Representatives and direct taxes shall be appointed among the several states which may be included within this Union according to their respective numbers, which shall be determined by adding the whole number of free persons, including those bound to servitude for a term of years, and excluding Indians not taxed, three-fifths of all other persons.

Section 9. "The emigration or importation of such persons as any of the States now existing shall think proper to admit, shall not be prohibited by the Congress prior to the year 1808; but a tax or duty may be imposed, not exceeding ten dollars on each person.

"The privilege of the writ of *habeas corpus* shall not be suspended, unless when, in cases of rebellion or invasion, the public safety may require it.

"No bill of attainder, or *ex post facto* laws, shall be passed.

Article III. Section 3. "Treason against the United States shall consist only in levying war against them, or in adhering to their enemies, giving them aid and comfort.

Article IV. Section 2. "The citizens of each State shall be entitled to all the privileges of citizens in the several States. No person held to service or labor in one State, under the laws thereof, escaping into another, shall, in consequence of any law or regulation therein, be discharged from such service or labor, but shall be delivered up on claim of the party to whom such service or labor may be due.

Section 3. "New States may be admitted by the Congress into this Union; but no new State shall be formed or erected within the jurisdiction of any other State; nor any State be formed by the junction of two or more States, or parts of States, without the consent of the legislatures of the States concerned, as well as of the Congress.

"The Congress shall have power to dispose of, and make all needful rules and regulations respecting the territory or other property belonging to the United States; and nothing in this Constitution shall be so construed as to prejudice any claims of the United

States, or of any particular State.

Section 4. "The United States shall guarantee to every State in this Union a republican form of government, and shall protect each of them against invasion; and on application of the legislature, or of the executive when legislature cannot be convened, against domestic violence.

Article VI. "This Constitution, and the laws of the United States which shall be made in pursuance thereof, and all the treaties made, or which shall be made, under the authority of the United States, shall be the supreme law of the land; and the judges in every State shall be bound thereby, anything in the Constitution or laws of any State to the contrary notwithstanding."

In so far as we are able to ascertain, the above quoted portions of the Federal Constitution are all the clauses of that instrument that have been at any time referred to as bearing upon the subject of Negro slavery.

It is worthy of note that the word "slave," or "slavery," was carefully evaded, and does not appear once in the entire instrument. Mr. Madison, who was a leading member of the Convention and who took full notes of its proceedings, tells us this silence was intentional—the Convention being unwilling that the organic law of the United States should directly sanction property rights in human beings.

In such passages as slaves are presumed to be contemplated they are uniformly designated as "persons," not as "property." Contemporary history affirms, that it was the opinion of a large number—perhaps half—of the delegates, that slavery could not long survive the stoppage of the slave-trade, which was expected to occur, and did actually occur, according to a clause of the Constitution, in 1808.

And so far as its legalization was concerned it came to an end in that year; but Negro captives continued to be smuggled in, in greater or smaller numbers, as long as the institution of slavery existed.

At the time of the framing of the Constitution Washington, Jefferson, and Patrick Henry held in common with many other leading citizens of Virginia that the institution of slavery was not only wrong from a moral standpoint, and contrary to the very principles upon which the government was founded, but that in the end it could result only in disaster to the masters. Think how much better would have been the material condition of the South to-day if the cruel practice could have passed from it with the throwing off of the British yoke, instead of holding to it, as she did, until compelled to desist by the horrible and devastating scourge of Civil War.

Jefferson denounced the whole system of slavery in the most emphatic terms, as fatal to manners and industry, and endangering the very principles on which the liberties of the state were founded—"A perpetual exercise of the most unremitting despotism on the one hand, and degrading submission on the other," said Jefferson.

Similar sentiments were entertained, and freely expressed, by Patrick Henry. "Would any one believe," he wrote, "that I am a master of slaves of my own purchase? I am drawn along by the general inconvenience of living here without them. I will not—I cannot justify it! I believe a time will come when an opportunity will be offered to abolish this lamentable evil. Everything we can do is to improve it, if it happens in our day; if not, let us transmit to our descendants, together with our slaves, a pity for their unhappy lot, and an abhorrence of slavery." These are some of the words of the illustrious Henry. Washington avowed that it was among his first wishes "to see some plan adopted by which slavery may be abolished by law." Unfortunately these generous and truthful sentiments were confined to a comparatively few liberal and enlightened men. The uneducated and unreflecting mass—especially in the South—did not share them.

The following interesting and consequential extract is from one of Jefferson's letters written to a friend in his old age:

"From those of a former generation who were in the fullness of age when I came into public life, I soon saw that nothing was to be hoped. Nursed and educated in the daily habit of seeing the degraded condition, both bodily and mentally, of these unfortunate beings, not reflecting that degredation was very much the work of themselves and their fathers, few had yet doubted that they were as legitimate subjects of property as their horses and cattle. The quiet and monotonous course of colonial life had been disturbed by no alarm and little reflection on the value of liberty, and when alarm was taken at an enterprise of their own, it was not easy to carry them the whole length of the principle which they invoked for themselves. In the first or second session of the legislature after I became a member, I drew to this subject the attention of Colonel Bland, one of the oldest, ablest, and most respectable members, and he undertook to move for certain moderate extension of the protection of the laws to these people. I seconded his motion, and, as a younger member was more spared in the debate; but he was denounced as an enemy to his country, and was treated with the greatest indecorum."

Partly on account of the principles enunciated in

the Declaration of Independence, upon which the Revolution was begun, the sentiments of Jefferson made considerable progress among the more enlightened strata of the people of Virginia, and as elsewhere related, she passed the act prohibiting the slave-trade, and conferred upon her citizens greater freedom of emancipation.   But apart from such meagre and even doubtful rights as the acts conferred upon the down-trodden, and much abused, Negro race, the conduct of Virginia, like that of other Southern states, and even the National government itself, was strongly contradictory to the asserted natural equality of mankind, and the expressed inalienable rights of every human being, as contained in the Constitution of Virginia, as well as in the Declaration of Independence, and the later Constitution of the United States.   In 1785 Washington complained in a letter to LaFayette that certain "petitions for the abolition of slavery, presented to the Virginia Legislature, could scarcely obtain a hearing."

Other states followed the example of Maryland and Virginia in prohibiting the further introduction of Negroes, stolen or captured in Africa, but we enter a profound protest against the absurd claims of partisans that such legislative acts are to be credited to these states as evidence of regard for the rights, or interests, of the black man.   On the contrary they were conceived in fear and selfishness, and enacted for the purpose of warding off the self-incurred penalties of murder and insurrection, as elsewhere pointed out.   In further substantiation of our view we give an extract from the preamble of an act of the North Carolina legislature, done in 1786, which is highly commendable in that it confesses its real motives in plain words.   This preamble declares the introduction of new captives from Africa to be "Of evil consequences and highly impolitic," and affixes a penalty of five pounds per head on all subsequent importations.

Thus we find that at the time of the adoption of the present Constitution the Southern section of the country was tightening rather than loosening its grasp upon the abhorrent practice of human chattel-ism, while in the North there was a distinct and growing belief that apart from any moral consider-ations, such gross violations of fundamental moral principles must necessarily entail and precipitate— in the not distant future—its inevitable penalties. And justice requires us to add that the more north-ernly states lacked the incentive of the South, in holding to slavery, for it had been found that the institution was little if at all profitable north of Maryland.

CHAPTER X

From the Adoption of the Constitution, in 1788, to the Year 1860—The Growing Sentiment in Opposition to Slavery

GREAT rejoicing throughout the new and sovereign states of America followed the glad tidings of ratification of the Constitution. The oppressed colonists had reluctantly declared, and triumphantly gained their independence, by the most perfect if not the most humane, of all arbitraments—that of arms—and were now securely bound together by ties of common interests and a government for mutual benefit.

The question of slavery was now to have a protracted period of comparative rest. The pressing needs of national quiet and time for physical rehabilitation after the seven years' struggle for freedom, deprived the people of time to discuss any question that could be postponed. Although living in a land of plenty the exigencies of war had so depleted the available supplies of all kinds that farming, home-making, and the setting in order the machinery of a new government, demanded all the energies of the people. The work of putting into practical operation the newly written Constitution was no easy task, especially when we remember that the coffers of the national treasury were empty. The makers of the new organic law of the land had only blazed an unbroken track through the tangles of an unknown political wilderness. It remained for American statesmen to clear the way for the ship of State and devise ways and means for the establishment and co-ordination of the several departments of government. Apparently on account of this pre-occupation, it was thirty years before the question of Negro slavery again came prominently to the front.

While those who took part in the framing of the Constitution evaded direct reference to Negro slavery, the majority were, nevertheless, opposed to it, and firmly believed that the instrument contained the disguised leaven which would in the end work the complete eradication of the evil; and in this their augury was accurate.

This majority consented to such clauses in the Constitution as we have quoted—making slavery temporarily possible—only because such a course was an acceptance of the lesser of evils; they did not endorse the practice in any other sense. The question which they had to decide was: Shall we accede to the demands for the continuation of slavery, or shall we fail to unite these disjointed states into a stable government, under a written Constitution. They saw that the Constitution must be adopted even at the cost of the perpetuation, or continuation, of slavery; so they minimized the necessary endorsation of human chattelism, and gained the complete triumph of the greatest conservative force for human rights the world has ever known.

There are some among us who teach that no compromise with justice can be right; but as the case in question aptly illustrates, such propaganda is the veriest sophistry. All sound logicians will assent to the axiom that when confronted with a choice of evils—which language implies that we cannot avoid a decision between them—it is the part of wisdom to accept the lesser, though we confess a certain amount of inherent injustice. The Constitution could never have been adopted on any other basis, for, as we have elsewhere seen, many of the colonies or states, while strenuously advocating the stoppage of the African trade, were holding fast to their human property-rights with the most unyielding tenacity. Particularly was this true of certain Southern states, with Virginia included in that group, although at times,—and through the influence of certain superior citizens—Virginia's legislative bodies were closely divided on the question.

Lincoln has said, in substance, that desire is determined by two factors, (1), the moral sense, and (2), self-interest. Of course a man of such renown and influence must have precedence for his utterances over ordinary mortals; but we believe, none-the-less, that if he had reversed these two controlling factors —giving *self-interest* preference over *moral sense*— he would have more correctly stated the case. It is also probable that if he had been writing sociology or philosophy, instead of making a political speech —in which he was, very laudably, trying to secure votes—he would have given "self-interest" precedence over what he calls "moral sense." If one would be sure of his ground in anticipating average human conduct he should reckon first with what the people—however erroneously—believe to be self-interest; then count all other influences as subordinate. On no other basis can we account for the support which slavery and the slave-trade received from Christianity. It is true, this modern alliance of Christianity with crime and atrocity is but a repetition of its earlier history; yet it is astounding that in this more enlightened age the pure morality and humble brotherly love, which Jesus so clearly taught, could be so distorted, and disguised, as to lend its support to a practice that so manifestly violated the lofty tenets of the noble Nazarene.

"Is it not a little surprising," said Patrick Henry, "that Christianity, whose chief excellency consists in softening the human heart, cherishing and improving its finer feelings, should encourage a practice so totally repugnant to the finer impressions of right and wrong? What adds to the wonder is that this abominable practice has been introduced in the most enlightened ages."

Although Jefferson was not a Christian in the religious sense, and was regarded as more or less materialistic—but more correctly agnostic—he penned these godly-sounding words in his "Notes on Virginia" in reference to the enslaved Negroes.

"Can the liberties of a nation be thought secure when we have removed their only firm basis, a conviction in the minds of the people that these liberties are of the gift of God; that they are not violated but with his wrath? Indeed I tremble for my country when I reflect that God is just; that His justice cannot sleep forever."

To review the names of these early statesmen—whether they be Northern or Southern—who unreservedly condemned the practice of slavery is to mention, practically, the entire list. They all saw its injustice, but the great mass of slave-holding people—who resided in the South—based their reasoning on self-interest—as they saw it—and overlooked or disregarded the moral aspect. It was not until we were well into the first quarter of the nineteenth century that Southern politicians began to whitewash, or attempt to whitewash, the practice of human chattelism.

There can be no question that many ordinary planters and other citizens, having known no higher state of society, and being incapable of independent reasoning, sincerely believed the system to be just and proper. A like regard for authority and teaching—irrespective of morality—among the great mass of our people, is equally amazing to-day.

Apart from the cutting off of the slave-trade—in so far as its legal status was concerned—by an act of Congress effective January 1, 1808, and the growing sentiment in favor of individual manumissions, the condition of the Negroes—who were largely coneentrated in the South—underwent little change during the thirty years from the ratification of the Constitution (1788) until the revival of political anti-slavery sentiment in 1818.

During this span of three decades of freedom from agitation the condition of the bondsmen, while slightly improved as to its cruelties, remained in every essential respect the same. One thing should be kept ever before the mind in scrutinizing the actual condition and environment of Negro slaves during the period with which this chapter has to do; which is, that the condition of slaves was as varied as was that of the masters. There were house-servants whose environment was at once comfortable, hygienic, and elevating. The position of valet to a Virginia gentleman was—to a man devoid of that sense of wounded pride, which we Anglo-Saxons would have felt—a most care-free and comfortable situation. Such servants really entered into nearly every pleasure of the master. In the chase, for instance, he was always a well mounted attendant, and by reason of his recent condition of savagery probably got more real enjoyment out of the sport than did the masters themselves.

As much may be said of the female attendants of the ladies; these maids were often humored and indulged, they literally dwelt in palaces and breathed the atmosphere of the finest Southern culture. Servants of this class, both men and women, were in every material sense far better off in slavery than in freedom, so long as the master was solvent; but they always stood in the grim shadow of financial reverses and bankruptcy on the part of their owners, which usually meant ruin to such favored servants along with the rest. They were then liable to fall into the hands of unscrupulous slave-traders or less indulgent masters and mistresses.

A much harder lot was that of the great mass of Southern slaves, generally known as field-hands; this class was usually entrusted to taskmasters or overseers, who in turn were responsible to the owners for requiring of them all the hard labor of which they were capable, and that too with the smallest possible outlay for their support. Hard indeed was the lot of the field-hand. They were on very much the same footing as the mules and oxen which they drove. It was considered highly improper, and in many localities illegal, to bestow upon them even the merest rudiments of education. They could rarely read or write—an accomplishment very common among house-servants. The overseers were permitted to flog and otherwise punish the toilers entrusted to their keeping, which subjected this class of slaves to the consequences of ill-nature, caprice, and an unusual degree of race hatred. These overseers were required—as a condition to their continued employment—to force the field-hands to their utmost capacity, and to turn their labors to financial profit. Many a frail or ill man has been forced or beaten to death under the exacting requirements.

This, however, was by no means the worst fate of the bondsmen, cruel and inhuman as it often was, it is not to be compared with the lot of that large number who, for one cause or another, sooner or later, fell into the hands of the slave-trader; for this was a veritable hell on earth, as all know who have given the Negro question even casual attention.

The occupation of slave-trading was so repulsive that it attracted, almost exclusively, the most degenerate individuals—men devoid of pity and incapable of remorse.

When a gentleman made an assignment—which was common—at least a portion of his human chattels were sold at auction and some purchased by the slave-trader. It makes one shudder for shame on the one hand, and for pity on the other, to call back to view the circumstances that this was more likely to be the fate of the maimed, aged, or pretty housemaid, than that of the stronger, grosser and pure-blooded Negroes. Those familiar with "Uncle Tom's Cabin" already have a vivid impression of the horrors of home slave-trade (as distinguished from African trade). To those who would know it better, but who have not read that admirable book, we unhesitatingly commend it.

There can be no doubt that many slave-holders and Southern planters were good to their slaves and cared tenderly for the aged and incapacitated, and threw a protecting arm about their young mulatto women; but, as we have shown, human nature is weak, and where we find *one* such master *many* there were who put self-interest so far above humanity, and the natural rights of the black man, that his treatment, on the whole varied, all the way from exacting requirements to the most outrageous debauchery and unendurable cruelty. If all masters could have possessed the character of General Robert E. Lee, slavery would still have been unjust and degrading, and contrary to the natural laws of human rights and human progress; but we are nevertheless, strongly inclined to the belief that manumission under such conditions would have been unfortunate for the weaker race.

Such conditions as have been depicted here (and much more perfectly in "Uncle Tom's Cabin") were not destined to last always. It was impossible that we should long continue to live under a Constitution founded on the enlightened and inspiring principles that "life, liberty, and the pursuit of happiness," are the inalienable natural rights of all, and at the same time hold millions of our fellow-men in absolute bondage. If men had held their peace in the face of such cruelties, figuratively speaking, the very stones would have cried out for justice.

Beginning about the year 1818 the question of property rights in human beings came again prominently to the front. Still more acute was the agitation over the demands of the South that slavery be extended into new territory.

In the National Congress of 1819 the famous case, afterwards known as the "Missouri Compromise," occupied a conspicuous place and was thoroughly debated on every side of the question. Those who opposed the admission of Missouri as a slave-state and contended for the constitutional power of Congress to impose conditions on admissions to statehood, based their argument on the provision of the Constitution which empowers Congress to admit new states into the Union. They construed this section to imply a discretionary power of Congress in the imposition of conditions. The opposition placed their main reliance in the doctrine of the equality of the states in the Federal system, and declared that Congress had no constitutional power to destroy that equality by imposing onerous conditions. There were a number of conflicting circumstances; among them was the admission, during the same year, of the state of Alabama, without any prohibition or restriction whatsoever upon slavery. The admission of Alabama as a sister state made the number of slave and free states equal. The admission of Missouri as a slave state would, therefore, again disturb the equilibrium.

During the debate on the application of Missouri for admission without restriction—which meant slave-state—the bill was amended on motion of James W. Talmage, of New York, in this language: "That the further introduction of slavery or involuntary servitude be prohibited, and that all children of slaves born within the state after the admission thereof in the Union shall be free." The bill thus amended passed the House Feb. 17, 1819, by a vote of eighty-seven to seventy-six. On March 2d, the Senate passed the bill without the amendment. Two days later Congress adjourned and the bill went over to the next session.

In December, 1819, another bill for the admission of Missouri was introduced, whereupon James W. Tayloe, of New York, offered an amendment in the House which provided that as a condition of admission the state should be required to adopt a constitution forever prohibiting slavery within its limits. This, of course, gave rise to a new and vigorous debate on the power of Congress to impose conditions upon the admission of a state into the Union. Meantime the perplexing situation was further complicated by the application of Maine for admission, with a constitution which expressly prohibited slavery in any form. The House promptly passed a bill admitting Maine, but when it came up for discussion in the Senate, in January, 1820, the friends of slavery in Missouri—who were in a majority in that branch—coupled the Maine bill with the Missouri bill to admit slavery in the latter and steadfastly refused to disconnect the two measures. In this situation the substance of the compromise was proposed by Senator Thomas, of Illinois, in an amendment which provided that Missouri should be admitted with a constitution allowing slavery, but that in all the rest of the Louisiana territory north of latitude 36° 30′ N., slavery or involuntary servitude should be forever prohibited. In this form the bill passed the Senate Feb. 18, 1820, and was coupled with the bill to admit Maine and sent to the House for concurrence. The House promptly refused to agree to this combination and the matter was then referred to a conference committee of the two Houses, which recommended that the Maine bill be passed separately and that the Missouri bill be passed with the Thomas amendment. To this report the House agreed and the separation of the bills as distinct subjects was renewed. The Southerners seem to have gained their main contention by securing the recognition of Congress that that body had no right or power, to impose such conditions as it saw fit upon any state as a prerequisite to its admission into the Union. President Monroe affixed his signature of approval to the Maine bill on March 3d, and to the Missouri bill on March 6, 1820.

This it would seem should have ended the controversy, but not so; for this was really but the beginning of the long fight for the natural rights of the black man, in common with all other men. The seeds of freedom implanted in the Declaration of Independence, and the leaven incorporated in the Constitution, in the words "life, liberty, and the pursuit of happiness,"—among other passages—were beginning to germinate; the wise could already detect the gray dawn of better days to come for the Negro race; while peering through the shades and shadows of two score years the lovers of human liberty and justice could discern, though dimly the "handwriting on the wall" which told them that the next generation would see the cruel yoke, forever lifted from the shoulders of the Negro slave.

Henry Clay—who was Speaker of the House at the time—though an outspoken abolitionist, exerted his strongest influence to bring about the compromise on the Missouri question.

In the next House this matter came up again with a new complication. Missouri presented her Constitution to Congress for its approval. This instrument contained a paragraph making it the duty of the Missouri legislature to prevent the immigration of free Negroes into the state. This seems to us so flagrantly contrary to the Federal Constitution that it is hard to understand how a state convention could have been so indiscreet as to have offered it—unless it was intended to irritate the anti-slavery element. This attempt at the prohibition of immigration of citizens of other states provoked a new outbreak of heated debate concerning the duty of the Federal Government, to protect the citizens of the several states in the exercise of their constitutional rights of citizenship in every other state; and it was only after heated, and protracted, negotiations that a bill was finally introduced providing that Missouri should be considered admitted as a state only after its legislature had declared that no law would ever be passed, nor any construction placed upon the obnoxious paragraph, justifying any law which might abridge, within Missouri, the rights guaranteed to all citizens by the Federal Constitution. The bill involving this second compromise was approved March 2, 1821, and in accordance with its terms Missouri became a commonwealth.

By this time the contest between North and South, with the issue of human slavery as its principal basis, was full on. Anti-slavery societies were formed all over the North. The rapidly expanding Northern press entered more and more vigorously into the agitation, while the anti-slavery societies circulated their literature broadcast, which comprised all manner of tracts, books, pamphlets, and business labels, denouncing slavery.

While many of the utterances and publications in the North were violent and ill considered, those of the South were perhaps even more so. Both sides had their conservatives who deplored these incendiary expressions, but the radicals greatly outnumbered them. Fuel was continually added to the sweeping flames that were rapidly preparing the sections for the final struggle.

The great majority of Southern slaves knew little or nothing of this discussion, and apparently cared less, as was so strikingly illustrated by their loyalty and devotion to their masters and their masters' families, during the four years of war, which held in the balance the issue of their liberty or their continued condition of slavery.

An incident which materially affected the situation —although condemned alike, of course, by thinking men both North and South—was the insurrection led by Nat Turner, a Negro slave, in Southampton County, Virginia. From the previous conduct of this Negro it is more than likely that he was a mental defect, or partial imbecile. He had all his life claimed to have had periodical visions and to have received messages or inspirations from the Deity.

His career, however, was short—beginning on the night of August 21, 1831, (Sunday) and ending some time the following (Monday) morning. He commenced, with four or five companions, by killing five members of his master's family in their beds. He then went from house to house killing all, sparing not even the smallest infants, and collecting recruits as he went; his work was completed by blotting out the lives of an entire neighborhood school. For this deed seventeen Negroes were executed. Turner himself, who went into hiding, was afterwards caught, tried, and hanged.

This sad occurrence, together with resentment by the slave-holding element throughout the South, caused a tightening of the masters' grasp, and produced renewed severity in disciplinary regulations of slaves. By his own deeds—or deeds of violence on the part of other slaves—together with the excesses of Northern extremists, the poor black man was subjected to unusual hardships. The first evidence of insubordination on the part of a slave was now cause sufficient to throw him into the hands of the trader at any sacrifice. Every passing year, and every succeeding political campaign, exhibited its increased sectional feeling and bitterness between North and South. In addition to all this the politicians—or many of them, as that class has always been wont to do—made political capital out of the strained relations, and thus continually fanned the flames of bitterness to greater, and renewed, violence.

While there were many good and sincere individuals on both sides during these turbulent times, we have long been persuaded that the North, and the Washington Government were on the side of greater justice. Viewed impartially no man can

justly censure those who opposed slavery and property rights in human beings, in this land of boasted
justice and freedom. On the other hand, the hot-
headed Southerners, biased by self-interest, as they
saw it, and influenced by established custom, were—
in the main—absolutely sincere in the position they
assumed.

We have often wondered if it would not have
been possible for the cooler heads on either side to
have gotten together, in the early fifties, and appointed a joint commission of carefully selected men
—of the caliber of Lee and Lincoln—and effected
a compromise on the basis of freedom to the
Negroes with some measure of compensation to the
masters. Then again,—when viewed in another
light,—it looks as if the tribunal of civil war may
have been best; for, had it been thus evaded, it
would probably have been precipitated later, when
its consequences would have been still more disastrous.

As we drew near to the half-century mark the impending conflict became more and more apparent.
The breach between the two sections widened with
every new phase which the situation assumed, and
increasing bitterness continually called forth greater
vituperation. The order of the day, from press,
pulpit, pamphlet, and politician, was crimination and
recrimination.

The semi-centennial was celebrated by the publication of a series of articles, in the National Era (a
newspaper published at Washington), entitled
"Uncle Tom's Cabin," by Harriet Beecher Stowe.
These articles were reproduced in book form in
1852. This world-renowned book gained the widest
circulation, and there can be no doubt that it hasten-
ed and precipitated—if it did not actually cause—

the final resort to armed violence. The author of that great book not only profited by many a copy read, but also by many burned, at the hands of pro-slave Southerners. In fact, to this day, a copy of that plea for freedom is occasionally consigned to the flames by indignant sons of Southern soldiers. Many attacks have been made upon the author; she has often been severely arraigned and condemned for advancing the diabolical theory, or charge, (in a magazine article entitled "The True Story of Lady Byron's Life") of incestuous intercourse between Lord Byron and his sister. Some believe her brilliant brother, Henry Ward Beecher, was the real author of "Uncle Tom's Cabin." However, and while we have nothing to do with the character of the author, it does seem that if her chief aim in life and literary efforts had been the moral uplift of the people she could have found a more suitable pabulum for popular consumption than such depths of degradation as incest.

Whatever bad there may, or may not, have been in her mental make-up she is the reputed author of "Uncle Tom's Cabin," which, in our judgment, is a great and highly commendable contribution to universal and perpetual human freedom. Her characters and descriptions were unquestionably exaggerated, but this is allowable and, in fact, admitted to be an essential feature of good story writing. Vivid word pictures in this class of literature serve to overcome the inherent dullness or deadness of written language; at best written language cannot be endowed with the animate character of spoken words.

From this time on, while wise men still hoped for peace, the impending struggle for supremacy was obviously a matter only of exact date; the signs of the times were unmistakable.

Without entering into unnecessary details, suffice it to say that in 1854 and the years immediately following, an angry contest arose over the question of slavery in Kansas and civil war actually broke out in that territory. The people of that entire country were greatly excited, and this matter went far to hurry on the crisis. The anti-slave people were resolved to prevent its extension into any of the then territories. To this end they formed the Republican party, which was defeated in the Presidential election of 1856, and the Democratic, pro-slave candidate Buchanan, was elected.

In the year 1857 the excited state of the entire country was greatly augmented by the decision in the historic Dred Scott case, which bears so directly upon the Negro question that we give a synopsis of it.

Many years prior to this decision a Negro slave named Dred Scott had been taken by his master, an army surgeon, from the slave state of Missouri to a military post in the free state of Illinois. Under the law his master's act in taking him to that state made him a freeman. But Scott did not assert his rights at the time and was later taken back to Missouri, and there sold with his wife and two children. His new master having struck him, Scott brought a suit for assault. Under Missouri law, a slave had no right to sue, but it was contended for Scott that he had been set free by being taken to Illinois and could not be again enslaved.

This question was at last carried to the Supreme Court of the United States, and in 1857 it was decided against Scott on the ground that no Negro of slave ancestry, whether he be a slave or not, had a citizen's right in the courts of the United States. The judges at the same time stated that slaves were property; that it was the duty of Congress to protect property, and, therefore, that Congress had no right to forbid slavery in the territories. This was in effect a decision that the Missouri Compromise had never been valid in law. This decision so inflamed both North and South as to make disunion (or attempted disunion) more certain, if possible, than before.

It will be observed that the biographer and historian espousing the side of the South always puts forward, in a conspicuous manner, the mooted question of States rights. And in many instances we agree with his assertions and postulations along this line. But the point we desire to make is, that such arguments are so frequently advanced as a means of justifying the South, and of enticing us away from the real crux of the whole situation—the question of human chattelism.

In substance,—and before both sides became so wrought up as to demand a contest of arms on general principles—the Federal Government said to the discontented South,—we are irretrievably opposed to the extension into new territory of the corrupting and unjust system of property rights in human beings; keep your slaves in the states where they now are, but make no attempt to extend the practice; and, while we cannot endorse you, we will regard the matter as without the Government's jurisdiction and attempt no interference.

The South's response to this was uniformly defiant and threatening; and amounted concretely to this: Mind your own business, keep your unsought advise and suggestions to yourself; we are sovereign States and propose to send our slave property where we please. As a means of enforcing this position, we warn those in control of the Federal Govern ment that we propose to brook no meddling, or interference; and if you dare attempt it we will exercise what we construe to be our constitutional rights, and retire from the Union.

Of course this ultimatum was never formerly delivered to the Federal authorities by embassy or other officials from Southern states; it merely expresses the general attitude of the whole Southern people.

In the early days of the Republic the opinion was very generally held that each of the states was sovereign, and that the Central Government was exclusively their agent, entrusted with the performance of certain limited and carefully-defined duties which they (the states) had entrusted to it. In fact this was the intention of the several states when they sent their representatives to the National Constitutional Convention. The fear that the Central Government would be empowered with too much authority, or that it would use the very strength which the states collectively granted to constitute a strong Central Government, and gradually usurp those greater powers which they (the states) so dearly cherished and believed they had reserved to themselves for all time.

In this apprehension their expressed fears have since proven to have been prophetic, for the history of this Government has been a steady march of encroachment and usurpation of both States rights and individual rights; until to-day we are but little if any better off as regards our freedom, than are those European States, whose deplorable example our wise fathers tried so hard to avoid. This has verily become a land of minority rule, and one in which the old story of the oppression, of the weak by the strong, is being repeated. The Central Government is controlled by the few who continually prey upon the many—and so it is with all minor departments of government. The whole situation so far as the National Government is concerned may be tersely summed up in the words,—tariff-fed trusts.

Fortunately for the contention of the South for States rights, Massachusetts and other Northern states had long since made the same contention, and came to the verge of secession before those common tariff and other interests arose, which turned that whole section strongly towards Nationalism.

No unbiased historian can justly claim that the South was wrong in her contention for governmental freedom of action. The trouble was precipitated by the immoral character of certain of her acts—notably that of slavery. If she had followed always the precept of the Prophet Micah—"Do justly, love mercy, and walk humbly with thy God"—there might never have been a division, and our common country might have been saved the calamity of civil war.

What might have been is often said to be the most idle and empty combination of words. But this conclusion is only the result of the most superficial thought; for the reflection,—*what might have been,*—has often led to nobler and wiser conduct.

But there were no pauses in the excited course of events at this time, reconciliation of differences was no longer to be numbered among the possible solutions of the burning slave question. It was a great, consuming parasite upon the moral and political affairs of the body politic.

It was now 1859 and the people were suddenly thrown into a convulsive state by the famous John Brown raid; an event which stirred afresh the passions of the nation from centre to circumference. As there have been many versions of this happening and frequent exaggerations we give the simple facts:

There lived a plain farmer in the northern part of New York—the Adirondack region—named John Brown, whose whole soul was devoted to the cause of the enslaved Negro. In 1856 Brown followed four of his grown sons to Kansas, taking with him a fifth son. There he became a leader of the Free State men. He came to Virginia with his sons and some others in 1859 to set in motion his long-planned scheme of Negro uprising or insurrection, which he believed would put an end to slavery. His plan seems to have been to arm and incite a number of Negro slaves, and thus frighten the South into repudiating the entire practice. Little did he know how small a place that word "fear" had with Southerners.

One October night, with a band of twelve or thirteen white men and five Negroes—eighteen in all—Brown seized the United States arsenal at Harpers Ferry, on the south bank of the Potomac River, which was then in Virginia—now West Virginia. Before he had done much damage, however, the Government had Colonel Robert E. Lee on the scene with troops to suppress him. Brown battered his way into the engine house of the arsenal, where he and his companions were barricaded. He was overpowered, captured, and later tried and convicted of treason and murder and subsequently hanged at Charlestown, Virginia—now West Virginia.*

---

*The various statements as to the exact number of men with John Brown at Harpers Ferry vary—some accounts say eighteen, others say twenty-one, so, while eighteen is most probable, we may safely say the number did not exceed twenty-one.

Mrs. Susan Pendleton Lee's school history of the United States

We do not think Brown was altogether responsible for what he did. His previous life shows conclusively that he was a mental defect, not even of average mentality, though a strong and healthy physical specimen. The fact that he was unable to support his family is evidence of his partial imbecility.

Utter failure was the result of everything he attempted. Personally we justify his execution on the ground that he was a menace to human society, but not on the ground that he knew better, and was willfully and knowingly immoral.

However, only the consequences of his act of inciting Negro insurrection is germane to our subject. To a very large extent the North made of Brown a hero and a martyr. The anti-slave element—very improperly — sympathized with the audacious scheme. In fact there is very strong ground for suspicion that Brown himself was incited to the deed by wealthy citizens of the North.

Of course this occurrence served to greatly excite and imbitter the South, which was already unable to view the situation dispassionately. Rightly or wrongly she held the North responsible for the John Brown raid, and was then quite ready to begin armed hostilities.

All this time the great body of Negroes remained obedient and faithful to their Southern masters. If they were conscious of the injustice of their condition of involuntary servitude, they certainly kept

---

says Brown had twenty-one white men, but this is probably only one of the *many errors* which that book contains. It is much more probable that the division of blacks and whites, as well as the total number which we give in the context, is correct.

The details of many historic events are found to differ slightly in these minor points—especially as regards numbers and dates.

their own counsel. It is our deliberate judgment that a very great majority of them were well contented with their hard lot, and that if they could have known and appreciated the difficulties of making their own way in the world, against the superior intelligence and bitter race prejudice of the white man, very many of them—had they been asked— would have elected to remain in slavery. This fact, however, is no justification of the system.

CHAPTER XI

Abraham Lincoln—The Civil War—The End of Slavery—Reconstruction

ABRAHAM LINCOLN, one of the greatest characters which our country has yet produced, now appears conspicuously upon the stage of national political events, which by this time had become closely centred around the Negro and his condition of enforced servitude. This uncouth Westerner was a broadminded man; a deep, accurate and profound thinker. His power of original, close and accurate thought, combined, as it was with sound judgment, has rarely been excelled. In addition to these virtues he was at once unbiased, altruistic, honest, just, peaceful, kindhearted, modest, calm and collected. It is rare indeed that we find a man—either in public or private life—so free from prejudices, so impartial in his judgments, and so capable of grasping and considering all sides of a question. It seems extraordinary that just at the moment of greatest need in the history of the country, this most capable man to meet all conditions should have arisen and been selected as the Chief Magistrate, and entrusted with the gravest public duties and responsibilities that ever fell upon the shoulders of mortal man. No wonder, with all the great and noble qualities which he embodied, and the crushing responsibilities which he assumed, he should be known to history as a man of sadness.

If the citizenship of both sides of the controversy

could have been sufficiently wise and magnanimous as to have entrusted all their differences to him alone, what a glorious, peaceful and profitable solution we would have had! Think of the horrible, blood-stained battlefields, the hundreds of thousands of widows and fatherless children left penniless to bemoan their irretrievable loss! Think of the stupendous amount of accumulated treasure ruthlessly squandered, and the subsequent political outrages and indignities which the South had to suffer, after the death of this big-hearted man, as a portion of the penalty for the wholesale enslavement of human beings; much of which might have been saved by the course suggested! There could have been no valid objection to such mediation, and results might have been even more beneficial if he and—that other God-like man—Robert E. Lee, had been jointly selected without conditions or restrictions to settle all differences.

As Pilate said when he was required to pass judgment upon Jesus, we can almost say of each of these great characters: "I find no fault in this man." General Lee's generosity and kindliness were a certain disadvantage to him from a military standpoint, in his high command of men; the very nature of the occupation called for severe and swift deeds of punishment and harshness, against which his great soul rebelled. But even if this be computed to him as a military imperfection it would have fitted him but the better for such a service as we have mentioned.

Lincoln loved his country, the Union, and his fellow-men; his foremost desire was to serve these interests. He thought property rights in human beings wrong, and frankly and publicly said so; but he sympathized with the South and loved it, even as he did the North. He never regarded the Negro equal to the white man, nor was he inclined to wrest him from the grasp of the South by force; but he did desire to see inaugurated some plan by which the race might gradually and ultimately gain its freedom; and he was uncompromisingly opposed to the extension of slavery into new territory. He did say that the country could not permanently endure part slave and part free; but he would never have consented to the arbitrament of civil war as a solution of the problem.

Here is an expression of his estimation of the Negro given during one of his famous debates with Judge Stephen A. Douglas, and before an audience of avowed abolitionists:

"My declaration upon this subject of Negro slavery may be misrepresented, but cannot be misunderstood. I have said that I do not understand the Declaration to mean that all men were created equal in all respects. They are not our equal in color, but I suppose that it does mean to declare that all men are equal in their right to 'life, liberty and the pursuit of happiness.' Certainly the Negro is not an equal in color—perhaps not in many other respects; still in the right to put into his mouth the bread that his own hands have earned, he is the equal of every other man, white or black. In pointing out that more has been given you, you cannot be justified in taking away the little that has been given him. All I ask for the Negro is that if you do not like him, let him alone. If God gave him but little, that little let him enjoy.

"What I would most desire would be the separation of the white and black races."

Because of Lincoln's real worth and greatness, no less than his intimate association with the national issues of his day, and the very large share which was his in solving for all time the vital question to Americans of property rights in human beings, we propose to quote freely in this chapter from his utterances concerning the Negro and what ought to be done in his behalf, and in the interest of the Union and the promotion of human happiness in the aggregate. The quotation above is taken from one of his famous debates with Douglas and is peculiarly fitting in this connection. Lincoln was, at that time, one of the national senatorial candidates—of the newly organized Republican party—in the state of Illinois. This was an anti-slavery party formed to serve the interests of those who were opposed to the extension of slavery into new territory. They also held that the framers of the Constitution did not believe the institution of slavery could long endure under its provision (which we have elsewhere shown to be historically true). This new party which Lincoln led also favored some plan—satisfactory to all interests concerned, so far as possible—by which the Negroes could gradually come into their rights as freemen. They did not, however, propose, teach or favor violence, or injustice, of any kind. Lincoln himself believed in some form of gradual change from slavery to freedom, such as freedom to those born after a certain date, and after they had attained to a certain age—say eighteen years. These circumstances made the utterances of the great statesman on this subject particularly significant; his audiences were eager to hear him condemn slavery and his position demanded that he give full expression to his convictions. For these reasons, and because his attitude has been so often and so grossly misrepresented in the Southern section of this country, we quote further and at some length from these speeches.

"I will say here,"—said the noble statesman, (in his reply to Douglas, in the first of their joint debates at Ottowa, Illinois, on August 21, 1858) "that I have no purpose, either directly or indirectly, to interfere with the institution of slavery in the States where it now exists. I believe I have no lawful right to do so, and I have no inclination to do so. I have no purpose to introduce political and social equality between the white and the black races. There is a physical difference between the two, which, in my judgment, will probably forever forbid their living together upon the footing of perfect equality; and inasmuch as it becomes a necessity that there must be a difference, I, as well as Judge Douglas, am in favor of the race to which I belong having the superior position. I have never said anything to the contrary, but I hold that, notwithstanding all this, there is no reason in the world why the Negro is not entitled to all the natural rights enumerated in the Declaration of Independence the right to life, liberty and the pursuit of happiness. I hold that he is as much entitled to these as the white man. I agree with Judge Douglas he is not my equal in many respects—certainly not in color, perhaps not in moral or intellectual endowment. But in the right to eat the bread, without the leave of anybody else, which his own hand earns, he is my equal and the equal of Judge Douglas, and the equal of every living man."

In this language Lincoln recognizes the fact that the Negro is conspicuously inferior to the white man, and affirms that he does not believe the Negro can ever enjoy equal social and political rights with the superior race. In this both science and experience have since shown him to be right. He also expressly repudiates any intention or desire to interfere with the South, although he believed that some change must and would, sooner or later, take place. He believed that this immoral institution was, and would continue to be, a bone of contention and a disturbing factor as long as it existed, and in all this most Southerners are now able to see that he was absolutely right. In the same speech he delivered himself in these words: "I leave it to you to say whether in the history of our government this question of slavery has not always failed to be a bond of union, and, on the contrary, been an apple of discord and an element of division to the house. I ask you to consider whether so long as the moral constitution of men's minds shall continue to be the same, after this generation and assemblage shall sink into the grave, and another race shall arise with the same moral and mental development we have—whether, if that institution is standing in the same irritating position in which it now is, it will not continue an element of division?"

Again and also in the same speech he says: "What is popular sovereignty? Is it the right of the people to have slavery or not have it, as they see fit, in the territories? I will state—and I have an able man to watch me (referring to Douglas)—my understanding is that popular sovereignty, now applied to the question of slavery, does allow the people of a territory to have slavery if they want to, but does not allow them not to have it if they do not want it. I do not mean that if this vast concourse of people were in a territory of the United States, any one of them would be obliged to have a slave if he did not want one; but I do say that, as I understand the Dred Scott decision, if any one man wants slaves, all the rest have no way of keeping that one man from holding them."

It was Lincoln's sincere desire and earnest aim to

settle the slave question peaceably, and in the interests of unity and good will among all the people of the different sections. He greatly desired that slavery should not be extended into new territory, and, —although he was morally opposed to the institution—he deplored and disdained any suggestion of interference with the institution in the Southern states. But, on the other hand, he was firmly convinced that it was the purpose of the Democratic party, both North and South, to extend slavery and make it national. This he was ever ready to resist, and fully determined that it should never come to pass, if it were possible for him to prevent it.

"Now, my friends,'" said Lincoln in this same address, "I wish you to attend for a little while to one or two other things in that Springfield speech. My main object was to show, so far as my humble ability was capable of showing to the people of this country, what I believe was the truth—that there was a tendency if not a conspiracy, among those who have engineered this slavery question for the last four or five years, to make slavery perpetual and universal in this nation."

Lincoln often refers to the fact that the great names so intimately associated with the Declaration of Independence and the National Constitution, represent men who thought substantially as he did upon this mighty question of slavery. But of all the great men of national fame who had preceded him Henry Clay was his decided favorite. His great admiration of Clay was continually cropping out in his public addresses. This high regard for Clay is well illustrated in this passage, which also throws more light upon his attitude towards slavery under the Constitution.

"Henry Clay, my beau ideal of a statesman, the

man for whom I fought all my humble life—Henry
Clay once said of a class of men who would repress
all tendencies to liberty and ultimate emancipation,
that they must, if they would do this, go back to the
era of our independence and muzzle the cannon
which thunders its annual joyous return; they must
blow out the moral lights around us; they must pene-
trate the human soul, and eradicate there the love of
liberty; and then, and not till then, could they perpetuate slavery in this country! To my thinking,
Judge Douglas is by his example and vast influence
doing that very thing in this community when he says
that the Negro has nothing in the Declaration of
Independence. Henry Clay plainly understood the
contrary. Judge Douglas is going back to the era
of our Revolution, and to the extent of his ability
muzzling the cannon which thunders its annual joyous return. When he invites any people willing to
have slavery, to establish it, he is blowing out the
moral lights around us. When he says he cares not
whether slavery is voted down or voted up—that it
is a sacred right of self-government—he is in my
judgment penetrating the human soul and eradica-
ting the light of reason and the love of liberty in
this American people."

In these views of this unique American statesman
we can but concur. He was honest, conservative
and right. If he had been told at this time that
conditions would so shape themselves that he would
emancipate all the Southern slaves by a single brief
edict, he would have believed his informant beside
himself. Lincoln greatly deplored the necessity for
his Emancipation Proclamation, and used every honorable means to avoid it. It at length, in 1862, became absolutely unavoidable as a war measure, and
his famous Emancipation Proclamation was issued

to take effect on the first day of January, 1863.

When Lincoln came into the Presidential office on the 4th of March, 1861, he found certain portions of the country in a state of actual rebellion. For a time he refused to recognize the appalling fact. He tried to persuade the South to listen to reason—but with no avail.

Most of the Southern people believed that any state had the right to retire from the Union at will. Many went so far as to regard the election of Mr. Lincoln as sufficient cause for the exercise of that right. South Carolina had taken the lead in this movement. That state called together a Constitutional Convention, and on the 20th day of December, 1860, an ordinance was passed, setting forth that South Carolina was no longer a state in the Union, but had resumed her independence. Conventions were called and similar Ordinances of Secession were adopted in January, 1861, by Mississippi, Florida, Alabama, Georgia and Louisiana. Texas took the same action in February of that year; Virginia hesitated, and the rest waited for her decision. As a matter of fact Virginia voted overwhelmingly against secession.

The six states which had seceded during December and January sent delegates to a convention held at Montgomery, Alabama, on February 4th, and there organized themselves into a new Republic, which they called the "Confederate States of America." This new Republic seized upon certain forts, arsenals, and other property of the United States Government. Fort Sumter was one of the few Southern strongholds remaining in possession of the United States. The North could not at first believe that all this was to be taken seriously. Major Anderson, who had retired from Fort Moultrie, because it could not be defended from the land side, was in command of Fort Sumter. He notified President Buchanan—a Democrat and Southern sympathizer—that that fort could not be held without re-enforcements of men and ammunition. At first the President would not act, fearing that such re-enforcements would precipitate a collision; but when Major Anderson informed him that batteries were building which threatened the fort's reduction, the re-enforcements were forwarded in an unarmed vessel, which was fired upon when she entered Charleston Harbor, and forced to return.

When Lincoln came into office—on the 4th of March, 1861—he took several weeks to decide what to do about Fort Sumter. Finally he determined to send a small fleet to Charleston with soldiers and provisions. At the same time he notified the Governor of South Carolina that the fleet would land no soldiers or ammunition unless attack was made—but would supply the fort with provisions only. The Confederates accepted this as a challenge and opened their batteries on the fort on the 12th of April. After a heavy bombardment it was surrendered on the following day. Lincoln had exhausted his resources for a peaceful solution, he had done all in his power to avert the contest. None deplored civil war more than he, but he was confronted with the stern reality of an actual state of war existing between the sections, precipitated by the notoriously hot-headed citizens of South Carolina. Under the solemn oath as Chief Executive of the United States he had no alternative, nothing was left to him but to accept the arbitrament of war with all its horrors.

In this situation he bravely addressed himself to the prosecution of the war, and the saving of the Union.

The idea originally held in a loose fashion by all the states, asserted strongly at one time by certain Northern states, and to this day firmly believed by a vast majority of Southern people; that in the adoption and ratification of the National Constitution they retained and reserved to themselves the right and privilege to repudiate that instrument and retire from the Union at will, seems to us—as it did to Lincoln—to have no real foundation in fact. A person, or a people, may have a most absolute belief in a thing without the slightest foundation for such a belief—this seems to have been the case as regards the right of states to withdraw from the Union. To our way of thinking there is not a clause or a word in the entire document that can be logically so construed as to contemplate its own abrogation, or confer upon, or reserve to, the several states, respectively, the right to disassociate themselves from that compact. The circumstance that the states firmly believed that such was their prerogative in no wise alters the verity.

Slavery was the real *gauge* of *battle,* but the *preservation* of the *Constitution* and the *saving* of the *Union* had now superseded former issues, and become uppermost in the mind of Lincoln. But for his extraordinary virtues this nation would have been hopelessly torn asunder, for during those trying years of war the North was more than once ready to abandon the contest and allow the South to go in peace.

As the years wore on, however, the physical exhaustion of the otherwise unyielding South became more and more apparent, and the passing of the iniquitous institution of slavery was seen to be merely a matter of time. The despised black man was to come into his natural and constitutional rights of freedom, and to enter the inglorious contest with the white man for the *survival of the fittest.*

The details of the war have no bearing upon the solution of the Negro question. The valor of the Southern soldier needs no commendation here; his splendid qualities in war and in peace are matters of universal admiration. The only way the misguided South was ever conquered was by Grant's system of attrition, which finally exhausted and completely prostrated the noble, and once stalwart, Confederacy. She no longer had men and money with which to prolong the struggle. The familiar and pathetic story of Lee's surrender at Appomattox on April 9, 1865, is fresh in the memories of all. His remnant of an army, which had shown in many battles the most indomitable spirit, was now reduced to absolute impotency. His men were in rags and starving. Lee's actual capitulation might possibly have been deferred for a time—possibly for a week—but when he saw that the last glimmering ray of hope had forever faded from the bosom of the lowering shades of adversity, his great soul would not sanction the ruthless sacrifice of the faithful few.

That the black man is wonderfully subject to his immediate environs and childlike in that his mental attitude can be readily moulded by his superiors, is nowhere better illustrated than in those turbulent times of Civil War and Reconstruction. While the master was bearing arms and doing battle to perpetuate the institution of human slavery, the servant was at home tenderly guarding and protecting the women and children he left behind, and tilling the soil to feed an army to fight against his freedom. The Negro slave really did not know what the great Civil War meant. He had a certain consciousness that war was being waged against his master, and was,in the habit of regarding any injury to the master as a loss to himself. His mental attitude towards the master and the family was very like that of the shepherd dog towards the flock; he had been trained to guard and serve them, and this he continued to do partly through force of habit.

The mental capacities of the Negro are limited—very limited, but it is far from truth to regard him as devoid of virtue. His commendable and uniform faithfulness during the trying period of Civil War is sufficient in itself to dispel this notion for all time. Properly trained, he was then, and is now, in many relations of life, a highly virtuous man. This wholesale condemnation of the race is unjustifiable and misleading. Treated with uniform kindness, and strict discipline and justice, he is capable of becoming a law-abiding and useful citizen in the menial occupations that do not require self-reliance and intellectual acumen. In these higher qualities, however, he is notoriously and almost uniformly deficient. The greatest honor and distinction which the Negro has ever won was his faithfulness and loyalty to his master's family during the Civil War. There seems to be no record of his violating this sacred trust. This was due to early training and environment, and should ever redown to the credit of the race.

Striking and significant was the sudden change that came over him as a result of the lamentable folly of Reconstruction times. The absurd policies and teachings of the North transformed him into an enemy of the white population and a perpetrator of brutal crime. The Negro was taught to hate his white neighbor and to oppose him in all matters of politics. In the first place all men who know the Negro character and his deficiencies will, we sup-

pose, agrée that it was unwise to suddenly confer
upon him the right of franchise. He had no conception of how to use it, and became the mere tool of
the corrupt politician. If the two races were to live
together—which was necessary—amity and a continuation of mutual toleration and respect, with
white domination, were the only possible conditions,
but amity and mutual respect were for a time at least
largely destroyed by the reign of the carpetbaggers;
nor have its direful consequences yet wholly disappeared. Second only to the conflict itself was the
chapter of errors committed at Washington by those
in authority after the assassination of Lincoln. President Johnson attempted to execute Lincoln's policies, but Congress took the matter out of his hands
and very naturally, but most unfortunately, and un-
wisely, attempted to cloth the Negro with powers
which he had not the remotest idea how to exercise,
and then infested the conquered territory with agents
who taught the Negro to despise and oppose the superior race with which he had to live. It was impossible that the consequences to both races could
be other than evil. Under this system the Negro
responded readily and became the bitter enemy, and
a constant source of danger to his white neighbors,
whom he had so recently defended and protected
with such commendable fidelity. Childlike, as regards his intellectual development he was, and is,
easy to influence for either good or bad. All these
facts are in perfect accord with our chapters on
Evidences of Mental Inferiority, and given the facts
there recorded, his conduct, under these given conditions might almost have been foretold.

The Negro was systematically taught that the
petty agents of the Government who had come
among them to protect them from re-enslavement

by Southern whites, were not only the agents of their deliverers, but the custodians of their rights as enfranchised freedmen. That their only hope was to set themselves in political opposition to their former masters, and assert, in every possible way, their social and political equality. Such pernicious doctrines poured continually into the ears of the feeble-minded Negro practically amounted to drenching the soil with his blood, and removing from his reach the very food which had ever been so abundant. He assumed an air, of self-importance and self-assertiveness, which engendered a new race prejudice, and caused the South to deny him the right of franchise, and to a large extent, the ordinary civil rights in the courts. In this state of feeling the very law of self-preservation came conspicuously to the front, and the prejudice came to be so strong that the cry of the black man for civil justice before Southern courts and juries was a mere farce—the verdict being pre-determined in many cases before the evidence was heard. Especially was this true in cases of personal violence. It was thoroughly understood that no jury would punish a respectable white man for violence toward a black one. In fact they were almost afraid to punish even a very bad white man because of the moral effect upon the Negroes wherever such facts were heralded.

If Lincoln had lived to complete the term in the White House upon which he had so recently entered, and Congress could have been forced or persuaded to allow him to deal with the question of Reconstruction—which he believed it his constitutional prerogative to do—by far the greater part of all these troubles would have been foreseen and averted. The South never lost a more useful friend. Bias and prejudice seem to have had no abode in the mind of this mighty statesman.

This colossal loss was as great to the black man as to the white, the greater to the South than to the North; for it was not only in accord with the longings of the great soul of Lincoln, but likewise his expressed desire and purpose, to calm the storm and smooth the paths of amity and industry for the two races, so widely separated by nature, but who were to work out their own salvation, side by side but separate, throughout the great Southland, which lay in waste and ruin at the feet of the great President.

When Johnson came into the office made vacant by the death of his superior officer, he attempted to execute the policies which he found so wisely planned, but the distracted Congress usurped the authority and entered upon that unreasoned programme of folly and retaliation.

The entire responsibility of solving the ugly problem then devolved upon the dominant Anglo-Saxon race of the South.

CHAPTER XII

The Beginning of the End

IT IS not the purpose of this work to offer such a solution of the *Negro problem* as we would like to see consummated, but to discern what—under the law of causation—is most likely to come of it. Our method of finding out what all passed ages and influences have foreordained, in this particular instance, is the careful consideration of all available evidence, or the application of the principle of induction and deduction. As we have stated in substance in one of the early chapters there would be no limit to human knowledge if it were possible to know perfectly all antecedent causes and the innumerable relations of their combinations and effects. This, however, is by no means possible, even in this isolated case; but we do entertain a strong belief that we can and do know enough—barring the intervention of some very great and totally unknown and unknowable future cause or influence—to presage the passing of the Negro race question as a pressing National sociological riddle.

Some have said that miscegenation with a more or less complete amalgamation is the only possible solution of the unique condition of two separate races —both in great numbers—occupying the same territory at the same time. Others have held that the mutual race hatred and conflict of interests would result in the violent extermination of the weaker by the stronger. Still others there are who believe that the wholesale deportation and colonization must, and will, sooner or later, be resorted to by the whites through the national government. While others yet believe that segregation in our midst—just as we have done the Amerind—is the tendency of the times.

All such propositions—for one cause or another seem to us alike ill founded; and in due season each of these theories will be taken up and considered.

As a preparation for the work in hand we have made a careful and systematic study of all available influences—both past and present—that operate to produce their effects upon the two races concerned in this problem. As a result of this study we shall attempt to offer the solution of the question, and the destiny of the Afro-American race. In other words, we put the questions involved to natural law, and sociological conditions, and strive to interpret aright their answers. The application of the science of philosophy to the study and right interpretation of facts is the method we employ.

When the war had become past history, and the Reconstruction period was over, the situation assumed a simpler and more natural aspect. Then it is that we catch the first glimpse of the natural *beginning of the end* of this *Negro problem*. Up to this time the artificial condition of slavery and mighty governmental influences and edicts had intervened to subvert the course of nature. Now this element of uncertainty had passed away. The white man was to exercise his *constitutional rights* of *life,*

---

*In this undertaking we are ever mindful of the fatal error of trying to conform facts to personal bias or pet theories, and at all times endeavor to rigidly exclude and evade this pitfall. Likewise we labor with a determination equally as vigilant not to refrain from stating the whole truth on any phase of the subject because its declaration may be displeasing in one quarter or another.

liberty and the *pursuit of happiness,* unmolested by the government, so long as he did not grossly interfere with his fellow-man in his rights to do the same. Likewise the Negro was free to pursue similar ends. Under these circumstances rapid and mutually beneficial adjustments of relations followed close upon one another, and, pleasing to relate, the ill-will engendered by the cruel Reconstruction misdeeds and abominable teachings has been steadily improving and rapidly disappearing ever since. But what was the really significant truth about this new situation? Happily enough the mutual relations of the races were to improve as regards ill-will and acts of violence; but the natural law of a struggle for existence and the consequent survival of the fittest were to be the determining factors from this time forward, and its inevitable consequences began to manifest themselves at once.

The Negro has never been able to compete successfully with the white man, and, for reasons already given he never can. As shown later, in a chapter devoted largely to statistics, the rate of Negro mortality doubled at once, as a consequence of his inability to conform to the laws of hygiene, even if he had known the meaning of that word and the simplest application of its law—which he did not— for the white man took for himself the lion's share of the fruits of the soil and required the Negro to consume his physical resources for a wage which would not supply him with a proper variety of food, and purchase for him comfortable clothing and hygienic lodgings. These and many other hardships have contributed to maintain the high rate of mortality inaugurated with this period of competition. We have it directly from one of the most expert statisticians in this country that after a careful investigation it is his deliberate conclusion that the time will come when the remainder of this Afro-American race will occupy a position among us similar to that of the American Indian and the European Gypsies—protected and preserved from absolute extermination; and we are fully prepared to concur in this conviction.

The Negro has not even had a fair chance to test his capacities. He has not been able to demand for himself a fair share of the higher mechanical arts and agricultural occupations, but has been shoved out, little by little, and forced to confine himself largely to the employments which the white man does not want—unskilled manual labor and poorly remunerative positions of drudgery; and there he will be kept if human nature remains what it now is, and has been, in all historic times.

There were a myriad of minor causes set in motion to militate against the numerical strength of the Negro by that series of events which placed him in active competition with one of the most resourceful races the world has yet produced. That he cannot long survive in anything like the relative proportions that existed at the close of the Reconstruction period is quite as certain as the assertion that two and two make four. This unequal contest is like a game of chess with a fully developed giant intellect, skilled in all the science and art of the game, sitting on the one side, and a child on the other, that scarcely knows a pawn from a king or queen. For the struggle for supremacy and financial gain, under a system of at least theoretical equality before the law, (in practice Negroes are not equal before the law) is verily a game between all who enter the contest. If the Negro had the same mental endowment as his adversary he could not even hope to win his share of laurels, for the white man would still have him handicapped by the vast power which great masses of accumulated wealth confer upon the possessor, the skill which comes only with experience, and the possession of governmental control, even down to the county district magistrate.

It is impractical to enumerate all the minor difficulties and defects with which the Negro has been confronted, and which he must continue to meet as long as the contest lasts; but in the chapters which follow, many of these will be brought out, and incontrovertible evidence adduced to sustain them.

Paradoxical though it be, the men who in these latter years came in increasing numbers from the North to the South, to establish for themselves homes in warmer climes, are the most aggressive and intolerant of all, when brought in close contact and competition with the Negro. They do not show the forbearance and patience with his stupidity and folly that the Southern-born man displays. When the settler from the North becomes acquainted with the many short-comings of the Negro he acquires a violent prejudice and animosity towards the race in general, to a degree almost unknown among the native whites. This is also shown to be more pronounced with the ignorant classes of laboring people, than is the case with the more cultivated settlers. In a word the man born and reared at the North cannot, after middle life, learn the Negro character, and how best to deal with it.

Many Northern enthusiasts formerly held—as some still do—that a little book-learning would enable the Negro to compete successfully with the Caucasian. There are even some Southern educational enthusiasts—with more learning than brains—who share this opinion; but a much larger number merely pretend it because it appears to be in one way or another, to their personal interest.

We do not mean to say that it is right or best to keep the vast Negro population in total ignorance of the merest rudiments of erudition, but we do assert that such education as is comprised in the three Rs is all the pure-blooded Negro should be given from the public fund—so far as book-learning is concerned. The rest should be a training of the hands, and that too in the so-called unskilled occupations; for the white man will not long allow him to hold the more remunerative positions.

We are perfectly aware that this position *may* and *will* be assailed with the citation of Negroes occupying positions in the learned professions—arts, sciences and literature—but when these are all summed up and compared with the total number of Southern blacks who are laborers, or with the total number of Southern whites occupying these higher positions, it will be seen that, in spite of the vast millions spent annually by both North and South for the education of the Negro, the number is so small as to be entirely without weight as an argument, and merely confirmatory of the conclusions to which our investigations have led us. Moreover that insignificant number of Negroes in the higher walks of life will be still further reduced, if we eliminate those having Anglo-Saxon blood in their veins.

No sooner had the government's agents of Reconstruction returned to their native heaths than the Southern Negroes began to realize that they had been deceived by these false friends, and for a brief time kept, by deception and artifice, verily in a land of make-believe. All nature assured them that, despite emancipation, the Declaration of Independence, the Constitution, with its thirteenth, fourteenth and fifteenth amendments, the bold assertion of certain Northern newspapers, periodicals, pamphlets and spoken words; to the effect that all men are born equal, etc., a white man is still a white man and a black man a black man for all that. They were quick to perceive that regardless of all assertions and man-made laws to the contrary, there is an infinitely higher power which has irrevocably decreed that the two races can never be equal in any true meaning of that term. Stern necessity taught the better class of Negroes that their only hope of salvation was to be found in the currying of friendship with the superior race and acceptance—with at least an apparent grace and satisfaction—of such menial occupation as the white man elected to assign them.

It was right and proper that the institution of slavery should have been abandoned, but it was un-fortunate that it could not have come to the South through its own volition, instead of being forced by the Northern half of our common country. The victory of the government was so complete in the great contest of arms that the rebellious South was powerless to offer further resistance. But on the other hand the North was equally powerless to con-fer upon the somewhat more than four millions of Negroes then residing in the South any sort of equality with their Anglo-Saxon neighbors. Nor is there now any power under heaven—short of abso-lute extermination of the superior race—that can prevent the practical elimination of the Negro in sufficient time by the natural law of the *survival of the fittest*. We do not wish to convey the idea that even in a thousand years the black man will have totally disappeared from these Southern states; but that in one-tenth part of that time the open contest of wits will have so reduced the black man, as re-

gards his relative numerical strength, that there will
no longer exist a serious Southern Negro problem.
That such influences are actively at work to-day is
abundantly shown by the evidence—when viewed
impartially—wherever we elect to study the question.

During the forty-five years of freedom many
Negroes have left the South and gone to the North
in the vain hope of discovering some of that equality
of which they have heard so much, only to find their
condition worsted rather than bettered. It is generally conceded that the economic and hygienic condition of the American Negro is much better in the
South than elsewhere; he is better suited to the climate and better understood. However, we cannot
always agree with Dr. Booker T. Washington in
what he has to say on this phase of the subject. For
instance, we find in his "Future of the American
Negro" this statement:

"Whatever other sins the South may be called
upon to bear, when it comes to business, pure and
simple, it is in the South that the Negro is given a
man's chance in the commercial world."

If he intends to say that the Negro's chance is better South than North he has spoken wisely, but if
he means by this assertion that in the South all the
avenues of commerce and trade are equally open to
both races his conclusion is singularly incorrect. This
latter condition never has and never will exist.
Again Dr. Washington says:

"Wherever the Negro has lost ground industrially in the South, it is not because there is prejudice
against him as a skilled laborer on the part of the
native Southern white man." The question arises
here as to the interpretation of the sense in which
he uses the word "prejudice." If he only intended

to say that in the South, and as a general proposition, there exists no abnormal, or unreasoned prejudice, his statement is fairly accurate, but if he means to tell us that as a skilled laborer he has an equal chance with the white man, the facts are overwhelmingly against him.   The truth that there is a very *strong* and *controlling race prejudice,* is, we believe, implicit throughout this work.   Any considerable knowledge of the operation of natural law reveals this without recourse to particular incidences.

We are therefore of the opinion that such statements from Dr. Washington are born of an abiding and commendable hopefulness and a controlling desire, rather than of calm and careful reasoning.

We have the greatest respect for Dr. Booker T. Washington and sincerely believe he has done and is doing a great work for his race; but we do not think he is always consistent in what he has to say.   He is cautious and moderate but by no means a profound philosopher.

If the reader will bear in mind the words which we have just quoted from Washington's "Future of the American Negro" and then consider carefully this further expression taken from the same work, we think this fact will be manifest.   After declaring that the absence of industrial prejudice at the South furnishes "the entering wedge for the solution of the race problem," he continues thus: "But too often when the white mechanic or factory operative from the North gets a hold, the trades-union soon follows, and the Negro is crowded to the wall."   Then he frankly admits that in no section of the South is the Negro "so strong in the matter of skilled labor as he was twenty years ago."

In the one instance he has said that there is no race prejudice in commercial and industrial pursuits in the South; and in the other that the Negro is driven out when the trades-unions appear. Now in the South these trades-unions are made up largely, of course, of Southern men.*

Is not this a race prejudice and a discrimination against the Negro race? He further contradicts his own statement that there is no race prejudice in Southern industries, and directly confirms the natural law—for which we are now contending—of continual warfare for the survival of the fittest, racially, as in all other respects, when he relates the fact that in no part of the South is the Negro as strong in matters of skilled labor as he was twenty years ago.

It is quite true that race prejudice is not the only factor in the warfare which is slowly but surely forcing the Negro out; for as we have seen in the chapters on *"Evidences of Mental Inferiority,"* the Negro is well known alike from everyday common sense observation and from a multitude of carefully collected scientific truths, to be very decidedly inferior to the Caucasian or Anglo-Saxon in every detail of his mental development, and therefore less capable than the white man of fighting the battles of life.

There probably is no essential difference in kind between the reason of the Negro and that of the white man, but there is a vast difference in degree in favor of the latter. It is this difference in degree of all the so-called higher faculties of mind that is to eliminate the black man as a serious competitor

---

*It is true that the trades-unions began originally in the North —just as nearly every great movement does—but it was manifestly destined to extend throughout the width and length of the entire country, as it has now done; and when it became securely established South it could be composed of none other than Southern men.

of the white man. Thus we unhesitatingly make the prophecy—speaking in general terms, and basing our words on well-ordered (scientific) knowledge—that the Negro is to be crowded out by the relentless hand of fate. Nor can we justly say that this is, in any true sense, chargeable to the white man, for it is an eternal decree of a power higher than Man. The black man is not responsible for being the most inferior variety of his species, nor did the white man entirely control the natural forces that made him (the white man) the most superior. Natural law has been doing the work for millions of years.

We are not introducing any new philosophy. To the zoologist and the botanist this process of the crowding out of a variety by other varieties, better fitted by the conditions which nature imposes, is matter of common occurrence. Hundreds of thousands of varieties of both plants and animals have in the past been eliminated in this manner.

To come back then to the details of this gradual elimination of the Negro, let us cite a few conspicuous factors—isolated incidences in a sense, but momentous factors nevertheless; illustrative of the general law of constant and resistless change.

We suppose it is generally known that the great Brotherhood of Locomotive Engineers, which is national in scope, is an organization composed exclusively of white men. Would this be true of the South, where ten million black people make their homes, if they were as capable as the white man? No, it is due primarily to the superior intelligence of the white man. As we understand this situation, the position of locomotive fireman has been in the past and—to some extent at least—still is, the training school of the practical engineer. There was a time in our own recollection when Negro firemen were common in these Southern states; they have gradually disappeared, until to-day it is rather unusual to see them, and a trades-union movement is on foot to eliminate them absolutely, if indeed, this crowding out process is not already an accomplished fact.

A little while ago, in a railroad car, we heard the conductor speak of a committee of railroad conductors and train hands, who were then in Washington negotiating with the heads of certain Southern railroad corporations for better hours, and better pay, among other things. Presently we engaged him in conversation, and for information plied him with questions concerning the details of the demands and the status of the case. Among other things, he said that the committee, which represented all the principal roads of the South, demanded that the pay of firemen be made uniform. We inquired into this and found that the railroads had been paying one price for white firemen and another for Negro firemen. We asked why the authorities did this. He said the railroads recognized the comparative inefficiency of the Negro, but that they were "so small" —as he expressed it—that they would often take the inferior Negro service in preference to the better, but more expensive, white service. We then asked him if he were sure the railroad superintendents would give up the practice of employing Negroes if the price were made uniform. To this he replied "We will attend to that end of it." "What will you do about this?" we inquired. "Wait and see," was his response, with a merry twinkle in his eye. He afterwards stated that no further action would probably be necessary to completely eliminate the Negro from this field; but that if the company continued to employ Negroes, a formal protest on the part of the organization would suffice, when the question of finance had been eliminated. The railroads subsequently granted all the demands of this trades-union committee.

This could not be construed as an act of Northern people through trades-unions, but an act of Southern people. Similar processes of elimination are everywhere operative. In this case the officers themselves recognized the inferiority of the Negro service by paying him a smaller wage. Then the trades-union demanded that the wage scale be made uniform in order that they might eliminate him. Back of all this and in addition to the financial side of the question was a strong race prejudice and an unwillingness to serve side by side with the Negro.

This crowding out of the Negro is not confined to the positions calling for skilled labor, but in many portions of the South it extends to nearly every occupation and subdivision of labor.

In the city of Richmond, Virginia, we have observed in the last twenty years the most marvelous change in this respect. Twenty years ago there were no white barbers in that city, ten years ago there were few compared with Negro barbers. To-day few Negro barbers are left, and these few have a preponderance of white blood. These so-called colored barbers are not equipped as well as the white barbers and their whole environment gives unmistakable evidence that their days are numbered; that they cannot hold their own against the superior intelligence of the white man in this field. Within the last twelve months the colored barber to the principal gentlemen's club of the city has disappeared and his place is now filled by a white man.

We no longer see colored carpenters and bricklayers in Richmond, or even in the country districts;

if they are employed at all their numbers are certainly small as compared with the white laborers in this field, or compared with twenty years ago. Delivery wagons are now largely driven by white men, and the same may be said as regards the running of elevators in public buildings. Likewise the street-cleaning force is exclusively white.

These changes are so rapid and conspicuous that we have often of late wondered what is to become of the Negroes now living—how they are to earn an honest livelihood. The only explanation is that our great country is developing so rapidly that perhaps all able-bodied men can find occupation of some sort in spite of their racial deficiencies and unequal opportunities. But this economic condition cannot last always, especially with our enormous annual influx of white foreign immigration.

The field of the Negro's activities is becoming so circumscribed as to constitute a cause of vital concern, and if the next few decades are to show a continuation of the present rate of displacement, we are unable to see how he can long continue to earn the bread essential to the nourishment of his body.

CHAPTER XIII

Negro Traits and Characteristics—Their Influence Upon the Race Question

SIR H. H. JOHNSTON, the noted administrator, writer and African explorer, tells us that the indigenous tribes of African Negroes exhibit an actual tendency towards *retrogression* rather than *advancement*. "In some respects," says Johnston, "I think the tendency of the Negro for several centuries past has been an actual retrograde one. As we come to read the unwritten history of Africa by researches into languages, manners, customs, traditions, we seem to see a backward rather than a forward movement going on for some thousand years past—a return toward the savage and even the brute."

This writer may possibly have overdrawn the picture, but what he has to say is confirmatory of what we have shown the race to be in former chapters, and at the same time enables us the better to account for *racial traits* and *characteristics* so conspicuous among our Afro-Amercian Negroes throughout the South.

There are several well-defined classes of Negroes in the Southern states and some, among the best class, display admirable qualities of thrift and foresight; but the great body of Negroes in the United States are little removed from Johnston's description of African tribal characteristics in their positive tendencies towards retrogression. This, too, is more marked now than it was twenty or thirty years ago and is especially noticeable in certain rural localities in the South, where voluntary segregations of the race have taken place almost to the exclusion of white population; and is unquestionably due largely to the fact that the generation of emancipated slaves was far superior in many ways to the later generations born in freedom.

Few Negroes are mentally capable of grasping the true meaning of freedom, and fewer still are able to conceive the relations which the race must ever bear to the dominant Anglo-American and the fact that industry, morality and frugality are inseparable conditions of substantial citizenship and public respect. A vague notion that liberty means license to idle away his time; to evade labor and effort; to avoid supplying the urgent needs of the white man for labor; and to indulge himself in the lowest depths of moral depravity; is the average Negro's conception of the privileges conferred by freedom and citizenship.

Unpopular though it may be, we are fully persuaded that much book-learning has proven to be a curse rather than a blessing to the Negro; and that it is to-day an active and potent influence in the solution of the Negro problem. If its present influence upon that race is to continue it will certainly constitute a contributing cause in his relative reduction in numerical strength, for too much book-learning absolutely disqualifies him as a laborer, and for the great mass of Negroes hard labor is the only hope of salvation. Most Negroes with a common school education look upon physical work as a disgraceful form of punishment, and when forced to it as a last resort—to drive starvation temporarily from the door—nothing can induce them to continue when they have a few dollars in hand. Neither their own nor their employers' interests will suffice to induce them to continue their labors until the pittance they possess has been consumed.

While all this is in perfect harmony with his lack of intelligence it is nevertheless positively alarming when considered from the standpoint of the welfare of that race. As we have already pointed out—and shall later show even more conclusively from statistical and other positive sources of information—the ultimate doom of the race as a serious American or Southern problem is in any event sealed and settled; but the present attitude of the great mass of Southern Negroes in positively refusing and evading work in every possible manner, is not only seriously crippling Southern commercial advancement—which, however, is only temporary, for they are being rapidly supplanted by white labor—but it is also threatening, and indeed actually producing among them a condition of starvation. Not a starvation in the sense of direct and sudden death from the total absence of food—although our alms-houses and other charitable institutions are well burdened with this class—but one of the contributing elements in an inordinate mortality rate; by virtue of the fact that this great body of worthless Negroes have an insufficient supply of a poor quality of food, and do not get a wholesome variety. This fact opens the way for the contraction and rapid progress of diseases of all kinds; which—as will presently be shown—are depleting the ranks of the race.

Those who, like ourselves, have carefully studied the Negro race from prehistoric times, or even those who have studied only the American side of the question, are already well aware of these truths; but unfortunately for the black race in the United States the great body of those big-hearted and generous Americans, who desire to befriend him with their philanthropic aid, are little informed as to the great basic truths that underlie the welfare and survival of the Negro. Unfortunately natural and artificial conditions have combined to supply the philanthropist with untrustworthy information regarding this whole subject. Many of the so-called authorities on this subject get their principal information by traveling about in splendidly equipped railroad trains, and banqueting with Negroes and whites who are far removed from the lowly—the real mass of our Negro population. It is without the range of average human nature—white or black—to be able, under this artificial environment, to gain an accurate and impartial mental concept of these great natural and artificial sociological problems. They, perforce, see things as they would *like* them *to be,* rather than just as they are *actually found to be* when considered in the cold concrete reality of causation and consequence.

The missionary, the educational enthusiast, the politician, the observer from foreign countries, while on the whole honest, are, nevertheless, all biased—each looking at things through glasses fitted for his special purpose, and ground for the work of magnifying those features of the conditions which it is pleasing to him to see in distorted proportions.

Of course it is natural also, for each of us to think that his opportunities for observing, as well as his capacities for interpreting the actual conditions, are superior to those of others. But it must, on the other hand, be confessed by all that the writer on this subject who has chanced not to come under any of these biasing influences is, in so much, a better interpreter of facts than those subjected to one or another of the special view-points referred to.

There are, as we have said, several distinct classes

of Negroes; a small class decidedly frugal and moral; a much larger class of small farmers and laborers, who are fairly prosperous; but more than half of all Negroes in southern United States are thriftless, aimless, lazy people; trying to evade occupation and consequently often seeking a livelihood through pilfering.

In nearly every section of the South it is a well-known fact—and, temporarily at least, a serious economic problem—that Negro labor is hard to get and unreliable even at high prices. Most Negroes had rather idle away their time than work for a dollar a day on the farm. There is probably not another country in the world where labor is plentiful and in demand, yet cannot be had for good wages. No other country could long continue to carry such a large class in comparative idleness; and the South will not do it always. This latter class of Negroes will be, and are now being, supplanted by a class of thrifty and industrious Northern and European settlers, willing and anxious to secure regular and profitable employment. It does not require a philosopher to foretell the inevitable consequence of this sociological condition.

If we were called upon to suggest the best means of aiding and protecting the Negro in health and happiness our reply would be,—give him from three to ten acres of land and just enough schooling to enable him to read, write and count. After a very careful and exhaustive study of this Negro question we feel absolutely certain that nothing could prove a greater blessing to the black man in America. The *possession* of a *small piece* of *land* does more to make of him a good and useful citizen than *all else* combined. He will never voluntarily sell it, but will apply himself to useful labor in order to hold it.

He appreciates the fact that if he does not pay his debts it will be taken from him. Such a possession gives him a little credit, and makes him feel the responsibility of citizenship—a relation of the individual to the body politic of which the great majority of Negroes seem totally unmindful.

We cannot emphasize this fact too strongly. To the wealthy citizens of the North, who regularly contribute money for the benefit of the Southern Negro, we would suggest a careful consideration and study of the frugality and respect which the possession of a very small tract of land brings to the Negro. This is well worth while if these wealthy citizens propose to continue to appropriate their substance for his benefit.

There is not a single besetting-sin of this intensely immoral race that is not ameliorated by this cause.

On the other hand, if he is given a good grammar school education, and sent out in the world, he is almost certain to seek idleness and evasion of useful and continuous labor. He apparently believes that gaudy clothing, an air of boisterousness, cigar smoking, and parading around public places—where he can be seen of all men—have a tendency to elevate him in the eyes of the superior race. This class of Negro, which is produced by educating him away from his sphere of usefulness, is a type that contributes largely to the startling criminal records of that race, both North and South.

However, we do not believe this advice will be heeded to any great extent, either by the Negro himself or by those white educators who seem to be intoxicated with book-learning. The teaching class seem to have totally forgotten the natural laws of supply and demand, which have decreed that even under the new labor-saving systems—which science

and invention have recently combined to so abundantly supply—a vast majority of the human race
must occupy themselves with manual labor.

What we say here is *applicable also to the white
race,*—which is *receiving too much book-learning
and too little manual training*—but applies with ten-
fold force to the inferior race which can never share
with the white man in the less laborious and more
desirable occupations.

We are perfectly aware that there are men and
women who think they have been well and accurately
informed on these subjects, who will say that the
past and present work and results of such institutions as Hampton and Tuskegee set at naught what
we have to say on this subject. And to this class we
would like to address a few observations.

In the assertion that many of the Negroes who
have graduated from these schools have been elevated to a higher and more useful, as well as a hap-
pier state of existence, we readily concur. But when
the further and wholesale inference is drawn that
such training schools when sufficiently extended—
so as to reach the great mass of Southern Negroes—
will prove to be the ultimate solution of this vast
problem, we must as positively dissent.

It has been abundantly proven, we think, that the
Negro is very greatly inferior mentally to the Caucasian, and that at least nine-tenths of the accomplishments attributed to that race are clearly due to
admixture of white blood. We venture the assertion that if it were possible to determine the ancestry
of all Hampton and Tuskegee graduates it would
be found that more than half of them are mulattoes,
with less than fifty per cent. Negro blood. It is a
universally admitted truth—by those familiar with
the Negro character—that few pure-bred Negroes

can be found who possess the essential qualities of a successful life in what are known as the higher walks, even if race prejudice could be eliminated. This would include not only ability to assimilate knowledge, but such mental faculties as originality, concentration, fixedness of purpose, powers of generalization, high moral character and broad conception of justice, and sufficient discrimination to enable him to make useful application of these faculties.

An exhaustive study of this subject, added to many years of close contact with the Southern Negro, justifies the assertion that when fifty such have been pointed, forty-nine can be shown to be cross-bred on the white man, although in many cases the color of the skin may bear little or no evidence of the fact.

Then, if it be admitted that the vast majority of so-called Negro graduates of these schools are part white, and that at least a part of their vaunted accomplishments may justly be computed to this cause, we would, for the time at least, let this feature of the contention rest.

Let us suppose for the sake of further argument that the point we have just made is not true at all, but that on the contrary every matriculate of Hampton and Tuskegee is required to present satisfactory evidence that he is a pure-blooded Negro. If this had actually been done it would not even then be reliable evidence of superior racial qualities; for, in the first place, it would be the superior few who would have been selected; and, in the second place, the results shown have been secured by such artificial means that it is unfair to introduce the same as evidence of comparative race merit.

Such results as these institutions have been able to show—and no one can doubt that those in charge have done their utmost to make a favorable show-ing—are the results of an almost unlimited supply of brains and money by the most superior specimens of the Caucasic race. If we may use a botanical ex-pression they are strictly hot-house products, forced to the utmost capacity of the material at hand by the brains and accumulated wealth of knowledge and money of the white man.

But if we would go further still and waive all this, and accept the most sanguine contentions of the most ardent advocate of Negro education and equality, the fact would still remain that if every multi-mil-lionaire in the United States were willing to spend his last dollar in an attempt to raise the standards of the Negro population of the South to the moral and mental requirements of Hampton and Tuskegee In-stitutes, the scheme could not be carried out on any such scale. Like the wonderful results and yields reported from experimental farms, it would prove to be contrary to the broader laws of general appli-cation.

While we do not place as much reliance in statisti-cal evidence, applied to broad sociological questions, as some appear to do, we recognize the fact that, when taken in its proper relation to other methods of study, it has its weight.

From this standpoint, and with such limitations as are here suggested, we offer the following chap-ter as support of what has been said in this and pre-vious chapters, and as—in its limited way—confirm-atory of what our study has led us to believe will prove to be the ultimate solution of a problem so vital to our great nation, and especially to that vast southeastern section, commonly known as the South-ern states.

CHAPTER XIV

The Testimony of Statistics to Numerical Retrogression Among Our Negro Population

IF THERE is any one line of scientific evidence more exact and conclusive in its testimony, and more important in its presentation of facts than others, that of statistics, when carefully collected, over an extensive period of time and from various sources, must be conceded this position.

It is none-the-less certain that to all, save those gifted with what may be termed a statistical mind, a multiplicity of tables and innumerable figures are extremely distasteful and laborious. In order to save the reader this useless labor, these tedious tables, with a few exceptions, will be omitted, and in their stead only reliable summaries of their contents, and interpretations of their significance, will be incorporated.

There is perhaps no single source of verifiable evidence offering stronger support to our assertion that the Negro Question is to solve itself—by natural causes—than that of statistics. It does not follow however that statistical evidence alone is by any means conclusive; for there are many chances of error both in collecting and in compiling, not to mention the possibility of starting with false premises in interpreting their concrete results.

Present methods of collecting statistics are by no means perfect or complete—many districts being unrepresented in important particulars—even if the work of collecting were perfect, which of course is not possible.

But in spite of all this, deductions from modern statistics by recognized experts are wonderfully accurate and trustworthy. They suffice for the conduct of business by the great insurance companies, and are relied upon by governments in caring for the public health.

None of the statistical evidence found in this chapter is utilized merely because it can be made to support our argument, and none excluded for the contrary reason; nor is a single item included which is not vouched for by the most reliable authority to be had.

RATE OF INCREASE OF NEGROES

On two tables, taken from the census reports for Continental United States from 1790 to 1900 A. D., inclusive, and published by Mr. Alfred Holt Stone, in "Studies in the American Race Problem," we find the following comment by the author:

"The last columns of Tables I and II show that the rate of increase of Negroes declined throughout the nineteenth century, that between 1880 and 1900 it was less than half of what it was between 1800 and 1820 and less than two-thirds of what it was between 1840 and 1860. It shows, therefore, that, if the future may be judged by the past, there is no warrant for the opinion of Mr. Washington, that the rate of increase in the future will be still greater than it has been."

The estimate of Mr. Page, that the year 2000 A. D. "will in all human probability" see from 60,000,-000 to 80,000,000 Negroes living in the United States, appears to be reached by projecting into the 1860 and 1880. If that rate were to persist through-future the rate of increase which prevailed between out the twentieth century, there would be 63,000,000 Negroes in the United States in 2000 A. D. If the rate shown by Table I for the decade 1890 to 1900 should persist, there would be 46,000,000 Negroes in the United States in 2000 A. D. If the rate shown by both tables for the twenty years, 1880 to 1900, should persist, there would be 38,000,000 Negroes in the United States in 2000 A. D. If the rate shown by Table II for 1890 to 1900 should persist, there would be about 35,000,000 Negroes in the United States in 2000 A. D. And, finally, if the rate shown in Table I for 1880 to 1890 should persist, there would then be about 31,500,000 Negroes.

"If it were admissible to assume that any rate of increase would persist throughout the twentieth century, it would be best to accept that for the twenty years between 1880 and 1900, because it is based on the longer period and involves no correction of census figures. But the history of the nineteenth century and what is known about the increase of population concur to testifying that the rate of increase is likely to dwindle, and that 38,000,000 Negroes in Continental United States in 2000 A. D. is much too large an estimate."

If we suppose for the sake of argument that the thirty-eight million rate—which must be admitted by all to be the maximum—persists and pertains in the year 2000 A. D., it would still be seen that at the present rate of increase of the white population the relative number of whites would, in less than a century, be vastly greater than at present. But as Mr. Stone points out, all evidence combines to assure us that there is to be a progressive decrease in the decennial increase of Negro population. Furthermore, we are convinced, by evidence contained in other chapters of our own work, that the rate of decrease is to be even more rapid than the evidence which Mr. Stone had before him at the time of his writing, justified him in indicating; although it is clear that Mr. Stone entertained a strong conviction, on general grounds, that the rate of Negro increase was to diminish faster than any figures at the time of his writing could be adduced to prove.

After formulating a table to show that the Negro population would, at the close of the present century, be less than 24,000,000 he continues as follows: "On the whole, I am disposed to believe that this assumption is as favorable to the Negro race as the facts warrant," et cetera.   A little further on Mr. Stone writes as follows:

"The rapid decline of white increase has been mentioned, and it might be thought that in this checking of Negro increase we have to do, not with a racial problem but a general problem of American population.   This is a superficial view.   It is true that the whites in the country as a whole, in spite of the swarms of immigrants who come to swell their numbers, are increasing at a slackening rate.   But nearly nine-tenths of the Negroes live in the Southern states, a region to which a small and dwindling proportion of our foreign-born population goes, and yet in the South the white population is growing with augmented rapidity.   The evidence for this surprising fact has been presented in the "Supplementary Analysis" of the Twelfth Census published in 1906, and need not be repeated.   Suffice it to say that, if each of the two races in the South should continue throughout the present century to increase at the rate that characterized it between 1880 and 1900, there would be in the South in 2000 A. D. about 33,000,000 Negroes and 155,000,000 whites, and the Negroes would constitute 17.6 per cent. of the population of the Southern States, in which they now constitute 32.4 per cent. Doubtless each of the above figures is much too large; but, if the checking of growth which will appear in each race shall effect them in such a way as to keep the ratio of their increase what it has been for twenty years—and I think this also is an assumption as favorable to the Negro as the facts will warrant—then the ratio of the above figures will be correct, and we may expect that the Negroes, who in 1800 were 35.0 per cent. of the population of the Southern states, who in 1840, when they were relatively most numerous, were 38.0 per cent., and who in 1900 had receded to 32.4 per cent., will continue to recede, and in 2000 A. D. are likely to be not more than 17.6 per cent. of the Southern population."

As a further proof of decreasing rate of increase in Negro population in the Southern states he refers to a table which he produces and proceeds:

"Table IV shows that in every Southern state the decline in the proportion of Negro children between 1880 and 1900 was much greater than the decline in the proportion of white children, and that with both races the proportion was smallest in the border states, and reached a very marked minimum in the District of Columbia. The last fact suggests that the proportion of Negro children may be very small in other cities. We have figures on this only for 1890 and 1900. They show that in the entire country, outside the large cities, the proportion of Negro children to 1,000 women fell from 672 in 1890 to 651 in 1900, or 21. But the proportion in the cities was 305 in 1890 and 260 in 1900, a decrease of 45. These figures show that the proportion of Negro children in cities is about two-fifths of the proportion in country districts, and has decreased in cities with more than twice the rapidity with which it has decreased in country districts."

Thus he brings out the forceful fact that *racially the Negro is consuming the candle of his existence at both ends.*

The study of statistics constantly impresses the student with the fact that while the death rate of both races is being gradually lowered, with the advance of improved methods of living which modern science affords, its benefits are increasingly greater among the whites than among the blacks. In other words, while the Negro is benefited by improved hygienic conditions that race does not receive its proportionate benefit; and that the difference in relative benefit from improved conditions of life is constantly increasing in favor of the white man. Another fact revealed by the systematic study of these figures, is that the growth of cities—in the South especially—while constantly depressing the birth-rate of all, uniformly affects the Negro birth-rate more than it does that of the white race. These conditions are at all times, and in all localities, conspicuously against the Negro race. These facts are well illustrated by this paragraph, which refers to a table on page 5 1 5 of Stone's "Studies in the American Race Problem:"

"Probably these figures warrant the inferences that the death-rate of each race has greatly decreased in the United States in fifty years, and that the decrease for the Negroes has been much less rapid, both absolutely and relatively to the initial amount, than the decrease for the whites. The death-rate indicated for Negroes in 1900 is more than five-sixths (84.6 per cent.) of what it was at the earlier period. That for whites is less than two-thirds (64.1 per cent.) of what it was at the same period. At the earliest date the death-rate of Negroes exceeded that of whites by 29.8 per cent. of the lower rate, in 1890 it exceeded the death-rate of whites by 56.5 per cent., and in 1900 by 71.5 per cent. Before the war the difference between the death-rates of Negroes and whites was 8.0, in 1900 it was 12.3. Clearly in this field the benefits of progress are accruing more to the white than to the Negro race, and the difference between the two races is growing."

The constant and increasing influx of Negroes to the cities tends greatly to augment the disparity between the numerical strength of the two races. Mr. Hoffman (now chief statistician to the Prudential Insurance Company of America) tells us in his "Race Traits and Tendencies of the American Negro'" published for the American Economic Society, by the Macmillan Company, that during the period from 1860 to 1890 the white population of the cities increased 94.11 per cent., as compared with an increase of 242.60 per cent. for the Negro during the same period. "This phenomenal increase in the colored population of Southern cities during the past thirty years is perhaps the most convincing evidence of the changed conditions at the South, as affecting the future of the colored population," says Hoffman.

On page 20 of his statistical work,—from which we are quoting—Mr. Hoffman makes the important point that if volitional segregation goes on in future as it has done in the past it will become a potent factor in checking advancement among the Negroes, and thereby increase the rate of decrease of the comparative Negro population of the country. "This tendency," he says, "if persisted in will probably in the end *prove disastrous to the advancement of the*

colored race, since there is but the slightest prospect
that the race will be lifted to a higher plane of civilization except by constant contact with the white
race."

The following table is copied from the United
States census report for 1900, and gives the comparative death-rate for blacks and whites according
to age:

| Age | | Death rate of | |
		White	Colored
0—4	....	49.7	118.5
5—14	....	4.1	9.8
15—24	....	5.9	15.6
25—34	....	8.6	16.9
35—44	....	11.1	21.0
45—64	....	21.5	36.7
65	....	86.0	108.6
All ages	....	17.3	29.6

This table is reproduced in the latest edition of
the New International Encyclopedia, in the article
on vital statistics, and commented on as follows:

"The death rate of the colored race in the United
States up to the age of twenty-five is approximately
about two and one-half times that of the whites, and
the difference between the two races is apparently
greatest between the ages of fifteen and twenty-five.
From that age the difference greatly declines, the
mortality of the colored being a little less than twice
that of the whites between the ages of twenty-five
and forty-five, and above the age of sixty-five exceeding that of the whites by only about one-

fourth."*

This table speaks for itself, no comment upon it is necessary.

Among living statisticians it may be doubted if there is one more impartial and able in every respect than Frederick L. Hoffman, from whom we have already quoted. Mr. Hoffman is a native born German; a fact greatly in his favor as an interpreter of statistics bearing on the American Negro Problem. Native Americans, of a generation now rapidly passing, who lived four years in the very midst of the fierce struggle between the Sections could scarcely have survived it without acquiring a decided leaning towards one side or the other and usually inherited a very fixed opinion either for or against the Negro. This is somewhat less true of a later generation, born since the passing of that contest; but of a man whose early influences were entirely foreign to the whole subject, and who did not come to this country until slavery was a matter of past history, no bias whatever can justly be ascribed.

The following quotation from Mr. Hoffman is a fair illustration of his conception of the tendency of the Negro race to decrease in numerical strength:

"The progress of the colored population in the United States, and more particularly in the Southern states, has for more than fifty years past been a matter of the most serious concern to those who have observed the results of the presence of a large and growing Negro population. The natural bond of

---

*Mr. Stone and other writers express the belief that this apparent lowering of the death-rate of very old Negroes is due in the first place to the fact that they are illiterate and usually give their ages too high; secondly, that they belong to a former generation of slaves and enjoyed a much lower death rate than those born in freedom.

sympathy existing between people of the same country, no matter how widely separated by language and nationality, cannot be proved to exist between the white and colored races of the United States. To-day after thirty years of freedom for the Negro in this country, and sixty years in the West Indies, the two races are farther apart than ever in their political and social relations. To-day, more than ever, the colored race of this country forms a distinct element and presents more than at any time in the past the most complicated and seemingly hopeless problem among those confronting the American people.

"It is, therefore, a matter of the utmost importance that the true condition of this population should be fully understood in all its intricate details, to eliminate every possible doubt as to the seriousness and importance of the problem to the people of the Southern states as well as the larger cities of the North and West. In the endless discussions that have been carried on for years past as to the condition and future of the colored people, the fact that there is a northern side to the question has never been fully taken into account. Only by means of a thorough analysis of all the data that make up the history of the colored race in this country can the true nature of the so-called 'Negro problem' be understood and the results of past experience be applied safely to the solution of the difficulties that now confront this country in dealing with the colored element.

"The most threatening danger, numerical supremacy, may be considered as having passed away, if indeed it ever existed in fact. Leaving aside the results of the eleventh census, which clearly proved a smaller increase in the colored population than in the native white, the material is abundant and will be fully presented in this monograph, to prove that, independent of the census returns the gradual decrease in the decennial growth of the colored population can be fully explained.

"During the past decade, however, according to the census returns the increase in the colored population of the southern states has been so much less than that of the white race, and so much less than the believers in Professor Gilliam's prediction had cause to expect, that the accuracy of the census has been disputed by many, even though they had no means whatever at their command of proving the truth of their charges. Since many of the tables and calculations in this paper are necessarily based on the eleventh census it may not be out of place for me to state that after the most careful analysis of the results in this and many other investigations I am convinced that the Eleventh Census was as carefully taken as any one of the ten preceding enumerations. This conviction is based principally on a study of the age distribution of the population, which is probably the most delicate test applicable to census work."

Professor Gilliam's prediction, referred to by Hoffman, is in part as follows:

Year	Estimated Negro Population
1880	6,000,000
1890	9,037,470
1900	12,000,000

From these faulty figures the conclusion was drawn (and the opinion widely circulated) that in seventy or eighty years—about the middle of this century—Negroes would greatly outnumber the whites in every Southern state.

In referring to the ill-founded estimation of Professor Gilliam and in pointing out that not only the high mortality rate (which Gilliam appears to have failed to reckon with), but every other cause of increase or decrease must be dealt with in these productions, Mr. Hoffman states, in substance, that only after a comprehensive and comparative study of the intricate details of the several contributing elements can the nature of the problem, as to the future of the Negro and his relation to the white race in this country be understood.

In the year 1900 the census report of the United States gave us in round numbers only 8,840,000 Negroes instead of Gilliam's estimated 12,000,000. If Gilliam's defective method of estimating population were brought down to 1910 it would give us a Negro population of something over 15,000,000; whereas the census will probably give a little more than 10,000,000.

This comparison of Gilliam's hypothetical figures with the actual census report of the United States, while illustrating the uselessness of attempts to foretell the increase of a race over a long period of years by methods which do not take into count all the conditions effecting such increase, also emphatically declares the rate of increase of the Negro population to be much less than that of native whites for the same territory—exclusive of the important item of white immigrations. At the same time there is shown a decreasing ratio of increase in Negro population, notwithstanding the fact that conditions of life are constantly improving and mortal statistics among the whole people correspondingly lowering.

The following is from the Twelfth Census of the United States, Volume I, Part I, Table LI, Pages

CXII and CXIII.

In order to avoid the introduction of a cumbersome mass of figures we omit the table and give only the summing up of its contents in the census report for 1900.

"The whole number of persons of Negro descent in 1890 was 7,488,788 as against a total in 1900, for the entire area of enumeration, of 8,840,789. This is an increase during the decade of 1,352,001, or 18.1 per cent. The whites have increased during the same period 11,824,604, or 21.4 per cent.

"These figures show that persons of Negro descent have not increased since 1890 relatively as fast as the whites, when the entire area of enumeration in 1900 is considered. If an examination is made of the relative increases of these two elements in the South Atlantic and South Central divisions, in which nearly nine-tenths of all the persons of Negro descent are found, the same conditions are apparent. In the South Atlantic division there has been an increase in the white population since 1890 of 19.9 per cent. as compared with an increase in the Negro population of 14.3 per cent., while in the South Central division the whites have increased during the same period 29.1 per cent. and the Negro element 19.9 per cent. If the comparison in these two divisions is extended to the several elements of the white population, it is seen that among the foreign whites there has not been so rapid a rate of increase as among persons of Negro descent, but that among the native whites, both of native and foreign parentage, the relative increase during the decade has been much greater. The percentage of increase in each element since 1890 in each of these two divisions are as follows:

"**South Atlantic Division.**—Native whites of native parentage, 20.5; native whites of foreign parentage, 20.9; foreign whites, 3.2; persons of Negro descent, 14.3.

South Central Division.—Native whites of native parentage, 29.2; native whites of foreign parentage, 39.5; foreign whites, 11; persons of Negro descent, 19.9.

The following table from the census report speaks volumes for the solution of the Negro problem on the basis of declining relative numbers:

TABLE I.

	Negroes	Percentage of Total Population of United States
1790	757,208	19.3
1800	1,002,037	18.9
1810	1,377,808	19.0
1820	1,771,656	18.4
1830	2,328,642	18.1
1840	2,873,648	16.8
1850	3,638,808	15.7
1860	4,441,830	14.1
1870	4,880,009	12.7
1880	6,580,793	13.1
1890	7,488,788	11.9
1900	8,840,789	11.6

It will be seen that this table covers a span of a hundred and ten years, and that the proportion of Negroes to the general population has declined for every decade since 1810 (there were extensive importations up to this time) except 1870-80; and it is now admitted that the apparent increase for the decade was due to faulty enumeration. If we accept these figures of the National Government (with the correction mentioned) as reasonably accurate—and we have no reason to doubt that they are—a simple calculation will show that the percentage of Negro population has decreased 7.7 per cent. since 1810 (which was two years after the Constitution permitted Congress to restrict importations), and that if we suppose that this general average of increase is to continue for the ninety-year period, from 1900 to 1990, the Negro population in the year 1990—or nearly eighty years hence—will amount to only 3.9 per cent. of our total population.

If this may be regarded as a fair basis of calculation we have still another surety for the soundness of our theory of a natural solution of the American race question. For when the total Negro population falls below three per cent. of the whole, there will be no serious race problem remaining, and in our calculations, based on strictly scientific methods, this will come to pass before the close of the present century.*

---

*It is a great disappointment not to be able to include the results of the census report for 1910 We have corresponded with the head of the department at Washington and he assures us that these calculations have not yet been made.

CHAPTER XV

Vital Statistics and a Summing Up of This and the Previous Chapter

H AVING seen that the American Negro is in a state of actual retrogression as regards his relative numerical strength, it is not without interest—as bearing directly upon our topic—to investigate the immediate relative causes of death.

Among the diseases most responsible for the high mortality rate of the Negro,—apart from the inordinate number of still-births, and deaths from infantile diseases (before the age of five years)—when mentioned in the order of greatest ravages, are tuberculosis, pneumonia and venereal disorders.

The death-rate of children serves well to illustrate the inherited vital forces, or lack of such forces, in the Negro race; and at the same time constitutes a very sensitive barometer of sanitary conditions. In every section of the country where records have been kept, still-births and infant deaths among Negroes greatly exceed those of the whites. In fact there are no statistics of infant mortality in this or any other country, that show such an alarming death-rate as that found among our Negro population. In Norway, for example, only about 10 per cent. of the children die before they reach one year old; in Russia the proportion rises to one-fourth, and in Bavaria to three-tenths. In Massachusetts about one-sixth of the children born die under one year of age. According to the figures of the Twelfth Census the death-rate of whites under one year of age in the whole country—as far as records have been kept—is 158 per thousand born, while that of Negroes is 372 per thousand, which latter is in excess of any other records found, and approximately two and one-half times greater than that of the white population for the same territory.

Hoffman very aptly states that the excessive infant mortality rate among our Negro population is to increase rather than decrease as compared with the white race, and that the figures abstracted from the Twelfth Census are sufficient in themselves to solve the race problem in sufficient time.

Before proceeding with the consideration of statistics bearing on the principal diseases that are so rapidly depleting the ranks of the Afro-American we would state that after the period of infancy is passed—although the statistician separates these diseases—it is nevertheless true that in many cases the given cause of death is really superinduced by pre-existing constitutional derangements. For instance, tuberculosis of the lungs—which is given as the most potent single factor in excessive adult Negro mortality rate—is frequently brought on by or associated with syphilis, scrofula or other depleting disorders consequent upon a life of debauchery. This, however, does not affect the conclusions drawn from the figures; for these conclusions would remain the same if the cause of death were given as a complication of diseases. More accurate diagnoses would result only in lowering the frightful records of tuberculosis and proportionately augmenting those of death from other causes.

At the time the Negro came into his freedom, and theoretical civil rights, that race was little, if at all, more prone to the great scourge of tuberculosis than was the Anglo-American. Since that time, however, and among the many splendid triumphs of science, there is to be recorded a great decrease in the percentage of deaths from this cause among the white population of the entire country. But despite the constant urging of those whose special duty it is to guard the public health, and the spending of millions for the benefit of the Negro, the totally unequal contest with the white man for existence has served to raise the former's mortality rate from tuberculosis and other pulmonary diseases, until to-day this single cause of death is one of the strongest factors in the process of elimination of the Negro as a *pressing National problem.*

The Negro death-rate from tuberculosis, when compared with the white death-rate from this cause, is found to be more than three to one.

Again Mr. Hoffman says:

"Considering now in particular the principal diseases to which the Negro is liable, and which will more clearly than any other series of facts bring out his race traits and tendencies, we shall first have to consider consumption as the most important of all. A volume could easily be written on this one disease and its influence on the destiny of the colored race. Few writers on Negro mortality have failed to discourse upon the excessive mortality due to this cause, and but few have failed to recognize the fact that this most dreaded of all diseases is constantly on the increase among the colored population of this country."

He then proceeds to give a number of comparative tables showing the startling loss of life among the Negroes from tuberculosis and other respiratory diseases.

Pneumonia, like consumption, in fact all diseases effecting the respiratory apparatus, are excessively prevalent among the colored race; presenting a record, wherever accurate statistics have been taken, of very nearly two to one, as compared with the white race. The following table is compiled by Hoffman, from the reports of Dr. Billings:

MORTALITY FROM PNEUMONIA IN SIX CITIES—1890

(Rate per 100,000 of Population)

	White	Colored
Baltimore, Md.	174.86	350.69
Washington, D. C.	140.28	352.72
New York, N. Y.	336.46	389.50
Brooklyn, N. Y.	277.47	493.33
Boston, Mass.	249.84	325.96
Philadelphia, Pa.	180.31	356.67

This table speaks for itself and shows that tuberculosis is not the only disease that has contributed to raise the Afro-American death-rate above that of any other people of whom any record has been made.

VENEREAL DISEASES

Closely allied to both tuberculosis and pneumonia among the Negro population of America are venereal diseases, all of which are more or less (so-called) constitutional diseases, with the exception of pneumonia, which is often superinduced by the pre-existence of one or more of the above named constitutional ailments.

In recent years the alarm for the survival of the Negro race in America has frequently been sounded by magazine writers, health officers and others, because of the proportions which venereal complaints have assumed, and the dreadful conditions existing as the entailed consequences of the wholesale violations of natural law. Perhaps nine-tenths of congenital blindness is attributable to this cause alone, as is also approximately the same proportion of rickets. If we may judge from the testimony of many medical men supported by such incomplete statistical evidence as can be had, it may well be doubted if one-fourth of our adult Negroes—regardless of sex—are free from some venereal trouble. Indeed we might have made this statement cover the population at all ages; for few Negro children are born without scrofulous tendencies, rickets, blindness, or other transmitted evidence of ancestral infection of this nature.

Most of the statistics bearing on this subject are collected from the medical records of examination of recruits for service in the army, especially during the Civil War. A table has been extracted from medical statistics of Provost Marshal General, Vol. I, Washington, 1875, which shows that the rejections of colored applicants for scrofula were 35.7 per cent., and for syphilis 181.6 per cent. in excess of white rejections for the same causes.

But we are not entirely without statistical evidence of the prevalence of these diseases in the Southern states in more recent years, and in civil life.

From the annual report of the State Board of Health of Alabama we take the following table:

DEATHS FROM SCROFULA AND VENEREAL DISEASES
AMONG THE WHITE AND COLORED
POPULATION OF ALABAMA

	Scrofula		Venereal Diseases	
	White	Colored	White	Colored
1890	10	23	3	37
1891	10	17	3	21
1892	8	12	3	24
1893	8	27	7	33
1894	8	15	6	40

These figures are supposed to represent the relative frequency and fatality of these diseases among the two races, but do not apply to sufficient numbers to be regarded as entirely accurate. Evidently such statistics were collected for only a certain portion of the population of Alabama, although nothing indicating this is given.

In the city of Charleston, South Carolina, during the years 1889-94 inclusive, the number of deaths from syphilis among the whites and colored was as 10 to 66 respectively, thus showing a most remarkable preponderance of this disease among Negroes.

This table shows the mortality rate per hundred thousand of population from scrofula and venereal diseases in Baltimore and Washington—1885-90.

	Scrofula		Venereal Diseases	
	Baltimore	Washington	Baltimore	Washington
White	6.12	5.28	3.06	5.89
Colored	29.09	38.39	13.29	23.89
Per cent. of excess of Negro mortality	375.3	627.1	344.3	305.6

Mr. Hoffman produces the table in his work on "Race Traits and Tendencies," and says: "In both cities, almost to the same degree, the Negro mortality from the causes under consideration exceeds that of the white population 344 to 627 per cent."

The same author then gives us this significant passage:

"It is because the disease is closely related to other diseases, principally consumption, and an excessive infant mortality, that the rapid increase of scrofula and venereal diseases among the freed people becomes a matter of the greatest social and economic importance.

"For the root of the evil lies in the fact of an immense amount of immorality, which is a race trait, and of which scrofula, syphilis, and even consumption are the inevitable consequences. So long as more than one-fourth (26.5 per cent. in 1894) of the births for the colored population of Washington are illegitimate,—a city in which we should expect to meet with the least amount of immorality and vice, in which at the same time only 2.6 per cent. of the births among the whites are illegitimate,—it is plain why we should meet with a mortality from scrofula and syphilis so largely in excess of that of the whites. And it is also plain now that we have reached the underlying causes of the excessive mortality from consumption and the enormous waste of child life. It is not in the condition of life, but in the race traits and tendencies that we find the causes of the excessive mortality. So long as these tendencies are persisted in, so long as immorality and vice are a habit of life of the vast majority of the colored population, the effect will be to increase the mortality by hereditary transmission of weak constitutions, and to lower still further the rate of natural increase until the births fall below the deaths, and gradual extinction results."

Mr. Hoffman has arrived at this conclusion from a totally different standpoint from that which first assured us that diminishing relative strength of the Negro population, and finally an actual falling off in its total numbers, would result in the *solution of this problem;* but he has only stated what becomes unmistakably apparent to any serious student of this mooted question.

However, this last quotation is not entirely free from error, one of which is embodied in this sentence: "It is not in the 'condition of life,' but in 'the race traits and tendencies' that we find the cause of excessive mortality." He should have said that a combination of conditions of life and race traits and tendencies are jointly responsible for this decadence of the race. Then again we of course do not endorse the statement to the extent of complete race extinction, but on this point Mr. Hoffman has modified this conviction as will be seen by a recent correspondence with him which is introduced in a later chapter.

There is material at hand to enable us to continue on indefinitely relating the high relative death-rate of the Afro-American as compared with the Caucasian or Anglo-Saxon, but sufficient has been given to demonstrate that the Negro, certainly in the Western Hemisphere, is decidedly deficient in the power of resistance to climatic influences and to various diseases. In other words the constitution of the white man is stronger and more capable of combating various climatic conditions and diseases than is that of the Negro. In Government reports the two to one death-rate—or nearly that proportion—holds good. But as we have stated this should not be regarded as due solely to race traits and tendencies, but to a combination of these qualities with his adverse or relatively unfavorable conditions of life. If Mr. Hoffman meant to include in his "Race Traits and Tendencies" the fact that nature has not endowed the Negro with the same mental capacities possessed by the Caucasian, then we must withdraw our criticism and agree with him on this point.

We have not been able to find a single writer,—with sound judgment—well informed on the subject, who does not confirm the salient facts and figures contained in this and the preceding chapter. They all admit that the Negro is inferior mentally and physically, and that he is unable to compete successfully with the white man.*

A SUMMING UP

In summing up the contents of this and the immediately preceding chapter, which have to do with statistical evidences of retrogression of the Negro, from the standpoint of health, we would call attention to the salient features contained.

The important fact is recorded in the outset that infant mortality is found to be two and one-half times greater among Negroes than among whites. Then it has been shown that throughout the nineteenth century the rate of increase of Negroes has steadily declined; that between 1880 and 1900 it was less than half of what it was between 1800 and 1820, and less than two-thirds of the rate pertaining between 1840 and 1860. Thus showing conclusively that there is not the slightest warrant for the expressed opinion of Dr. Booker T. Washington that the rate of increase in the future will be greater than it has been in the past. But contrariwise, if all signs and statistics combined have any significance whatsoever, the Negro rate of increase is to decline steadily until finally the birth-rate will fall below the death-rate; and in time the remnant of the race will cease to attract attention, because of its decreasing actual numbers. It is true that when immigrations of white population are eliminated it can be shown by the

_____

*Note that we say—with sound judgment—"well informed writers," for there is practically every imaginable view recorded by some.

figures that the rate of increase from native white births is slackening and that there is substantial ground for the wide-spread belief that Negroes multiply faster than whites; or, more correctly, perhaps, that Negroes give birth to more children; but when the inordinate infant death-rate among our Negro population is taken into account, it is clearly shown that the total number of white children surviving to years of maturity, productiveness and reproductiveness, is vastly greater than that of the black race. (It is true that more Negro children are born, in proportion to relative numbers of adults, but the excess is by no means as great as many appear to believe).

The next point made is that while the Negro receives some benefit—as shown by statistics—from the improved conditions of life, which the rapid advance in the science of hygiene affords, he is not benefited proportionately, to the extent that the white race is. The proper interpretation of this condition is that every scientific advance which improves the health and increases the average period of existence of the whole people, tends to solve the Negro problem by diminishing the relative numerical strength of that race.

The next point made is that while the rapid growth of population of Southern cities decreases the birth-rate of all, it effects the Negro birth-rate far more than that of the white population. And the fact must also be interpreted as portending the ultimate solution of the problem by a widening ratio of blacks to whites.

Then we have found that prior to the Civil War the difference between the death-rates of blacks and whites was 8.0, and that in 1900 it was 12.3; thus showing that our progress has been far more advantageous to the white than to the colored race; that every influence of time and change redowns to the detriment of the Afro-American, trying to work out his salvation under the unique conditions of a vast number of a lower race, first imported into an alien country as slaves, and later emancipated, possessed of theoretical civil and political rights, and left to his own meagre capacities and devices, to compete, on unequal and disadvantageous terms, with superior numbers of Anglo-Americans.

The marked tendency of the black race to segregation, which, as all are agreed, means death to development and progress of that race is the next important point made. It has been repeatedly shown that so long as the Negro is shut off from close daily contact with a superior race he is. absolutely incapable of progress or advancement of any sort whatsoever.   Indeed it is recognized and demonstrated truth that when segregated, and totally separated from contact with other races a retrograde movement uniformly takes place among Negro peoples.

In the densely populated Negro districts of certain Southern states this segregation has taken place to a very considerable extent, and there is no evidence of its cessation; but on the contrary it is increasing according to all the evidence available.

Near the end of Chapter XIV we have produced a table showing the constant decrease in Negro population for every decennial enumeration since 1810. The total falling off in percentage of Negro population during the ninety-year period was found to be 7.7 per cent. If this average rate of decrease in per cent. of population be projected into the future for a like period it gives us a percentage of Negro population in the year 1990 of 3.9 per cent. which as a matter of fact, if present tendencies and influences are to continue will be very decidedly smaller than the figures would indicate.

In the conclusion of the chapter it is observed that such an insignificant percentage of Negroes as will then exist in the United States is too small to attract attention as a serious race problem. Thus we have led up to the natural ending of the mooted Negro question, without any purposeful interference or intervention by the whites, for the accomplishment of that end.

In the present chapter we have shown some of the records of the diseases that carry the Negro mortality rate so far above that of the white race; and it is noticed that deep-seated racial traits and characteristics are responsible for the prevalence of these diseases; all of which may be included in the fact that the Negro has not been improved in past ages—either physically or mentally—as has been his Caucasic brother. Thus in the struggle for existence—which means the survival of the fittest—all processes of reason combine with the most accurate observations to declare the former the unfit variety.

Attention has also been called to the fact that there is no justification for attempts to separate his present condition from his past environment, or his natural inheritances from his long line of stupid, indifferent, savage, ancestors. Past history of the Negro variety of human kind and present-day traits and tendencies are inseparable.

CHAPTER XVI

Negro Criminality

CRIMINALITY is defined as the science which treats of the *causes and nature of crime,* but it hardly seems justifiable to class this branch of investigation as a science at all in its present state of development. The causes or influences lying behind the many kinds and degrees of crime are as varied and complex as those which have produced Man himself, and many of these causes—certainly many of their combinations—must forever be consigned to that class of phenomena which consist of so great a multiplicity of impressions or influences operating during such vast ages as to place them beyond the power of Man to disentangle.

Its separate study and classification as a science is of very recent development and is largely due to Cesare Lombroso, an Italian professor in the University of Turin, who in 1876 published a book entitled, "L'uomo delinquente" (Criminal Man), which attracted the attention of the civilized world. Since its appearance the subject has received wide attention, and been treated at length by eminent scientists—jurists, physicians, sociologists, economists—and those who have to do, in various capacities, with the conduct of criminal institutions. But on nearly every branch of the subject there exists the widest variation of opinion, therefore it is hardly proper to speak of criminality as belonging to science, which means exact knowledge, or known facts arranged in their proper relation to one another. If criminality is subject to such treatment at all it is certainly in a very limited way, and even then there exists the widest diversity of opinion as to the correctness of its formulas.

The fact that the Negro is inferior racially implies that he is also more criminal. However, in addition to his unbroken line of savage and barbarian ancestry—up to the time our American Negro became a chattel—there are other extenuating circumstances with which the Negro should be credited. It is true that he has perpetrated many crimes for which he has never been punished, but it is likewise true that he has been punished for a great deal of crime which he has not committed.*

Justice to the despised black man necessitates this admission. Nor is it fair to compare his criminal records with those of the whites. Not that such records should be either suppressed or minimized, but that he has actually been charged with and punished for more than his fair share of the total amount of crime committed in the political communities in which he resides. In other words the white man more frequently evades detection, and when detected and convicted usually suffers a less severe penalty.

The white race makes the laws, interprets and executes them. Could it be reasonably supposed, under the circumstances, and in the very face of a violent race prejudice, that the weaker race has received, and is receiving, an equal degree of legal

---

*We do not say this in a spirit of criticism, but as historically true. With a population of nine million Negroes in the Southern states it is essential to rule them rigidly, and to inflict severe and speedy punishments. This is not only essential for the protection of the whites, but broadly considered best for the blacks.

benefits and immunities? It is not within the bounds of human nature. And if it were, expediency would discountenance such a course so long as the race question continues to occupy the vital position it now does, and has done, for more than a century past.

As has often been observed—in answer to Utopian theories in pro-Negro discourses regarding the equality or supremacy of Negroes in the South— we are not, in this instance, dealing with *theories* of any kind, but with a most *serious condition*. We must handle the situation according to necessities, and in favor of absolute and unwavering supremacy of the Anglo-Saxon. Sir H. H. Johnston in a recent publication complained bitterly of the stern and rigid social regulations applied uniformly to our nine million Southern Negroes; apparently forgetting that not long since the United States Government was memorialized by certain American Negroes to the effect that in Johannesburg and its environs—a British community, where a similar condition exists —they were not allowed to use the sidewalks, but required to confine themselves to the middle of the streets.

Our government very properly declined to notice the matter further than to state that no effort would be made to interfere with this police regulation.

The broad and logical view of this South African regulation is that such a requirement, found necessary by a great people like the British, is probably essential for the highest interests of the superior race in that locality. And Sir H. H. Johnston might profit by reflecting upon this more generous attitude of Americans.

In a paper entitled "Contrasts and Parallels," Mr. Walter F. Wilcox says:

"The Southern people have lately been told by an

eminent American scholar that they cannot hope to solve the race problem, or any other problem, 'until they first learn the real barbarism of their social standards.' My reply to this generous suggestion would be similar to Mr. Blaine's answer, as Secretary of State, to the then Italian Minister on a certain important occasion when the latter found fault with our confusing dual system of state and Federal governments. It was to the effect that he was sorry, but really did not believe we would make any immediate change. It is not safe to generalize about the attitude of fifteen or twenty millions of people on the subject. But I feel that I can say that the white people of the South believe that where two races, as widely different as are the white and black, live together in large masses, public policy requires the observance of certain regulations in the ordering of the social relations between the two. Furthermore, they are entirely satisfied that every single instance of disregard of these established regulations is of harmful tendency, through force of suggestion and example, and this without the least reference whatever to the social station of the parties immediately concerned, or to the effect upon them as individuals. It matters very little how we may designate this—as *race prejudice, social barbarism,* or what not. There it is, and it is grounded upon no such feeling as may be dismissed with a sneer. It is based upon high considerations of the general welfare of the state, and rises to the dignity of a fixed canon of social and public law."

It may be regarded rude by some to refuse to break bread with Negroes, but we venture the opinion that it is no less impolite and discourteous than requiring him to walk in the middle of the street, and denying him the use of the sidewalks.

Wherever there are great masses of an inferior race closely associated with a superior, the fittest must survive and exercise supervision and control over the unfit. This is an inflexible and irrevocable decree of mankind in all ages and in all lands, reinforced and uniformly supported by natural law throughout the entire kingdom of living things; a law superior to ordinary interpretations of justice. None familiar with the Negro character can reasonably assert that it is safe to grant him all the social and political prerogatives possessed by the master class, and this axiom may be applied in South Africa, Brazil, Southern states of America or elsewhere, without requiring the slightest qualification.

And when we come to view the situation thus abstractly it becomes more than ever apparent that our treatment of the Negro, since emancipation, has been greatly tempered by the improved moral concept of our own race. If the situation had been reversed, and the black race had possessed all the powers of government and numerical domination, but retained its racial qualities, the white man would have long since been blotted from the face of the earth, so far as these Southern states are concerned.

Returning then to the question of relative criminal records in the United States, it should be borne in mind that North as well as South the Negro does not receive the same awards of justice before the law that are visited upon the superior race.

Passing strange it is, after the many protests and lamentations that have come out of the North, regarding the ill-use and abuse of the Negro in the South, criminal records show that in proportion to numerical strength, he is more frequently and more severely punished in the North than elsewhere. However, we have at least a partial explanation of this to be presented later which relieves that section to some extent at least of the charge of unduly harsh treatment.

There is before us a mass of evidence from sundry sources and by various writers, showing the high percentage of crimes committed by Negroes in all parts of the United States; but it seems best to present only a brief statement of the general facts, thus avoiding prolixity in the presentation of a mere phase of our subject.

For example, in the city of Charleston, South Carolina, where the colored population constitutes 56.39 per cent. of the whole, it was found in a recent investigation of records that the proportion of colored among the male criminals was 65.58 per cent. and among females 79.19 per cent. For the period 1889-94 inclusive, Negroes are shown, in a table compiled by Mr. Hoffman from police records of Charleston, to be responsible for 82.09 per cent. of homicides, and out of 18 cases of rape 17 were committed by Negroes. For crimes against property the Negro is likewise shown to be responsible for more than 90 per cent.

In the Northern states, in the year 1890, there were twelve white prisoners to every ten thousand whites, and sixty-nine Negro prisoners to every ten thousand Negroes. In the state of New York, and in proportion to their numbers, the Negroes contributed over five times as many as did the whites to the prison population.

The number of Negro prisoners in Southern states increased, between 1880 and 1890, twenty-nine per cent., while the white prisoners increased only 8 per cent. During this same period, and in states where slavery was never introduced, white prisoners increased 7 per cent. faster than the white population, while Negro prisoners increased 39 per cent. faster than the Negro population.   Thus the increase in Negro criminality exceeded the increase of white criminality—if we may judge from the number of prisoners—more in the North than in the South.

In the few figures here presented, which have been selected as reflecting the general average of the great mass which are accessible to all who care to take the trouble to review them, it will be seen that the rate of Negro criminality is much higher than that of the white race, and that the increase is astonishingly more rapid throughout the length and breadth of the country.   The state of New York serves as a fair type of conditions elsewhere.

Writing on this subject Mr. Hoffman says:

"All the tables for various states and cities confirm the census data, and show without exception that the criminality of the Negro exceeds that of any other race of any numerical importance in this country."

Our explanation of the fact that Negroes commit, or are convicted of more crimes in the North than in the South, is twofold; first a large proportion of the Negroes residing in Northern states are mulattoes, a class known to be more criminal than the pure-blooded Negro.   Moreover, many of these migratory Negroes leave their homes because of their criminal tendencies.   Their roamings being often due to compulsion rather than choice.   Secondly, law is better enforced in the North and fewer criminals escape its vigilance.   It may well be added that in all sections the white man takes his race prejudice with him when he is called upon to sit in the jury box, and, contrary to the contemplation and declaration of the law, too frequently considers the Negro prisoner guilty until he has abundantly established his innocence, thus transferring the burden of proof—in the case of the Negro—from the commonwealth to the prisoner.

There is still one other factor which should be recorded in considering the excessively high criminal records of the Negro. Sociology has established the fact that poverty greatly increases the percentage of crime among a people, and that this is made even more conspicuous where great poverty and great riches exist in close proximity. This fact not only serves to relieve the Negro of some of his burden of crime in the South, but applies with even more force in the North, where the white population is richer and the Negro relatively poorer.

But when all these allowances have been made, the criminal tendencies and records of the Negro still stand out in bold relief, as necessary consequences of the fact that he is racially and mentally the most inferior branch of the human species.

This tendency to commit crime constitutes an important element in his elimination, not that the number actually killed or imprisoned is sufficiently large to perceptibly influence the question, but that prison life is detrimental to subsequent progress and health; and racial reputation for crime and unreliability militate against improvement in the conditions of the race.

CHAPTER XVII

Negro Education

AND there are also many other things which Jesus said, the which, if they should be written every one, I suppose that even the world itself could not contain the books that should be written."

The idea conveyed in this quotation from scripture aptly illustrates the feeling of hopelessness experienced when we attempt to wade through the deluge of writings on the subject of Negro education. The world somehow manages to contain them without giving evidence of the slightest interference with her annual journey around the sun, or serious disturbance of her diurnal and nocturnal alternations, but woe be unto the man who attempts to read them every one!

Fortunately there is no occasion here to enter thus deeply into the subject; suffice it to consider briefly the expediency of educating the Negro at all, and if so, to what extent, and in what direction. It is expected that the views here expressed will excite the hearty displeasure and disapproval of some, for it is quite impossible that all of those living in sections of this vast country where there is no Negro question should entertain the same opinions in this regard, as do some of those living in the midst of this black population.

It is our deliberate opinion—and we trust it is not founded on prejudice—that the ability to read, write and count a little is all the book-learning the Negro should receive from the public fund.

Considered from the standpoint of the Negro this is best, although he does not see it so; and when regarded in its relation to the highest interests of the Southern white man, it is likewise sufficient; but if the latter's conduct is any criterion of his conviction he also disagrees with this conclusion. However, we do not believe that the action of the South can be taken as the will of her people. They are to some extent influenced by Northern opinion, but to a much greater degree dragged along by an intrenched minority, consisting of its own school authorities and other politicians, who (whether correctly or incorrectly) have little regard for the will of their constituency. We are strongly inclined to the belief that if the people could lift the weight which suppresses the truth, it would be found that a majority of our Southern people are willing to go quite as far in this direction as we have gone.

Humble submission to the powers that be and close attention to practices of frugality, in the restricted field which he is destined to continue to occupy, is the only sensible course for the Southern Negro to pursue. If he is not satisfied with this, it is bad policy for him to make known his discontent. If he wants more he should seek it elsewhere and in communities having no Negro problem to consider.

As a matter of plain fact, the Negro race is not capable of utilizing more book-learning than such as we have suggested, and even if it were the South is not the place—according to the fixed canons of its people—for the Negro to step up higher. We do not think the natural limitations here ascribed to the colored race are too drastic, but, be that as it may, the fact will ever remain inviolate, that the Southern people at heart discountenance any attempt to elevate the Negro. Whatever he may be in the eyes of those who do not live in his presence, he is a Negro and a servile race in the judgment of every right-thinking Southern white man. We simply do not want any equality of any kind whatsoever, and, moreover, will not tolerate it. The truth is the South grits her teeth at the very suggestion of equality, and swears a solemn vow, as a unit, that such shall never come to pass so long as the white race survives.

What then, may we ask, is there for the Negro to gain? What does he aspire to, unless he hopes to become mentally so strong as to be able to break down and override the race doctrine of the whites, and force amalgamation upon an unwilling people? If ultimate equality and intermarriage be his aim, it is too preposterous to debate; and if he expects to abide the inflexible decree of the master race there can be no justification for his wholesale education in directions which can never be of practical utility, even if he possessed the required natural fitness.

In spite of what has just been said the further truth remains that the Southern white man is the best friend the Negro has. The industrious Southern Negro, who shows no inclination to depart from the established paths of recognized inferiority to the white race, while retaining a jealous regard for his own respectability in his proper sphere, is well thought of and treated with generosity and esteem by all. But just in proportion to his departure from this demeanor the Negro suffers hardships. When he dons his gaudy clothing and parades the highways and other public places on work days, with a characteristic air of importance and self-assertiveness, declining labor and regular occupation as beneath his dignity, his lot becomes hard indeed.

This latter class is the type that schooling tends

to produce. They are reared in an atmosphere that has no part with manual labor as a means of subsistence, and when school days are over they are not willing to start afresh to learn the vocations and habits of life, which both God and man have decreed, shall occupy the days and hours of their humble lives.

He lacks the power of reason and foresight to enable him to discern the inevitable. He is unable mentally to grasp the situation, and, for this deplorable state, those who have forced book-learning upon him are largely responsible. The higher occupations are not open to him, but he seems to live in a forlorn hope that sooner or later every barrier—both natural and artificial—will be suddenly burned away. He despises all white men, partly because their lot seems easier than his, and partly by reason of a natural race prejudice. Thus in many cases he sooner or later falls into prison and serves to increase the criminal records of his race, and augment the burdens of the white man.

Therefore we are willing to go on record as declaring that very little book-learning is all that Southern Negroes really need. That certainly within the area of extensive Negro population, even a good common school education is a decided disadvantage to the Negro, and a constant menace to the white race. That such education militates against the progress of the Southern Negro and against the survival of his race in that locality.

There is nothing for the educated Negro to do. A goodly number become teachers in Negro schools, and others become Negro preachers, the latter class being generally regarded as a burden and a disturbing element to both races.

Negroes are not capable of building up and conducting large business enterprises, certainly not capable of doing so in competition with the white man, a relation and an obstacle which must continue to confront the Southern Negro to the end of time if need be.

Out of the total ten million blacks and mulattoes we doubt if there are as many as one thousand—including all those that have even a slight strain of Negro blood—conducting independent manufacturing plants of any considerable size.

If we had ten thousand Negroes in the Southern states at the heads of as many large manufacturing plants, built up by their own energies and brains, while employing no other than Negro labor, there would exist a demand for a considerable number of men and women of that race with a good common school education. We would then also have a Negro question on our hands showing little tendency to solve itself, and the future of these Southern states would be gloomy indeed; but, fortunately for both races no such situation exists and there is not the slightest prospect of such a complication arising in the future. The difference in the capacities of the two races is wide enough to absolutely guarantee this.

Hard labor in hot climates is the natural and proper sphere of the American Negro, and there he must ever remain. Natural law has fitted him admirably for this position, and his superiors are more than willing to concede it to him; but after spending the formative years of his existence in public and private schools he is no longer content to accept it. Whereas if he is trained to it from early youth up—as in former days—he will continue in it, and there find the highest degree of happiness of which that race is capable. This wholesale schooling of

Negroes in totally impractical studies is a perversion of nature and a crime against humanity.

Nature has so ordered things that at least 75 per cent. of mankind even under our modern system,—made possible by the great advances in science and discovery—must continue to occupy the field of manual labor. Only a small portion of the highest races can escape this necessity. Is it probable that any considerable portion of our Southern Negro population can ever escape this inexorable law? Is it logical to suppose that the superior race will take upon its own shoulders the burden of digging out of the soil the bread with which to feed both itself and the inferior race, dwelling in its midst? Is it not natural and more likely that the former race will compel the latter—who is better fitted in the warm climates of its principal habitation—to do proportionately more of this labor? If this be sound reasoning our contention that few Negroes are benefited by more schooling than the mere ability to read and write—certainly in a direction that trains them away from labor—cannot be gainsayed.

Are we then to continue to educate an inferior race for positions which they are mentally incapable of filling, and which positions do not, and probably never will, exist to be occupied by the Negro?

Thus we are confronted with the absurd spectacle of the white race squandering hundreds of millions of dollars for the education of the most inferior of all races—occupying the same territory at the same time with itself—to fill positions which do not exist, or to occupy stations which they themselves (the whites) have entirely too large a percentage of educated population to supply, and self-preservation demands that they retain.

This wholesale reversal of the natural order of

things can never be artificially accomplished to any great extent, or for any prolonged period. The combined civil and military powers of this entire nation could not force this state of affairs upon the Southern states. Moreover if the white race were wilfully to turn over to the Negro population of the South every clerkship in the entire land, economic necessities of both races would compel the whites to reoccupy them almost immediately.

The *sudden elevation* of the Negro is *impossible,* it cannot be accomplished until he has had *many generations* of *slight mental improvement* in which to make of him a capable and reliable race; and long before this comes to pass he will have been practically eliminated from the American continent by peaceful and natural causes.

Is it not time we should pause in this distracted policy, and calmly ask ourselves the question, whither are we tending, and what must be the inevitable consequence of detaining the entire youth of our Negro population in public and private schools until the formative period of life is past? Thus making of them a people unable to acquire the habits of earning a living and improving their physical and material condition by honest labor, while having nothing else to offer them.

The continuation of such a policy can only serve to increase criminal records, make bad hygienic conditions worse, and expedite the ultimate reduction of the race. Therefore we hold, and unhesitatingly declare, that the only logical course for the Negro to pursue is frugality and contentment in voluntary servitude, or independent pursuit of the manual occupations.

At present the governing race is consuming millions of dollars annually—not to mention brains and energies directly expended in this cause—in a fruit-less, hopeless, endeavor to elevate the most inferior of all races to a higher and unnatural plane; and this too to the detriment alike of both races.

If the Negro has any proper place among us it is in that field which he occupied before emancipation, minus his bonds of slavery, of course. He was then, in a certain sense, an economic advantage as a lab-orer in the cotton, rice and tobacco fields of the sunny South. He was then comparatively healthy and contented, while under the present regime he is alarmingly unhealthy, notoriously discontented, and a frightful economic and social burden to the com-munity in which he resides. Even among our own Southern citizens few indeed have any conception of the real magnitude of the burden which we are carrying, for the purpose of educating the Negro population away from its only sphere of useful em-ployment; not to mention the fact that every dollar thus invested (beyond teaching him to read, write, and count) serves to make bad matters worse, at least so far as the present and immediate future are concerned.

These facts may be illustrated by the present sit-uation in Virginia; speaking roughly Virginia is spending annually—from its public fund alone—more than a million dollars for the literary educa-tion of her Negroes; and every cent of this vast sum comes directly from the pockets of her white citi-zens. Not one penny is contributed by the Negro for his own education. This does not take into ac-count the sums voluntarily contributed by her white citizens, or citizens of other states. Private citizens of the North probably contribute a larger sum; and what is the result?—a weaning of the Negro youth away from his only field of usefulness, and an annual increase in his criminal records with additionaι deficits in criminal expenses to be met by the white race.

We have stated that the Negro does not contribute any portion of the money expended for his education. The explanation is that his criminal expenses exceed his tax receipts,—of every kind and description—in fact the total expenditures in this direction are more than double his total tax receipts. Thus in addition to the sums mentioned as expended by the whites for Negro education in Virginia, it becomes necessary to meet a large annual deficit because of his criminal expenses. And the more we contribute to his education the higher runs his record of crime. Appalling as are the facts in Virginia, it but illustrates existing conditions in every other state, and every large city of the entire country having a considerable Negro population.

And this exposition of fact, when considered in its proper relation to other portions of this work, we believe more than justifies our conclusion that we are wrong in educating the Negro beyond the merest rudiments of erudition, such as are commonly included in the three Rs.

If the remainder of this money could be judiciously expended in the purchase of small tracts of land and simple equipments for its cultivation, a great deal of good instead of much harm, as at present, might be accomplished; at least in so far as the condition of the Negro is concerned.

As the matter stands to-day we are giving the Negro book-learning for which he contributes no part of the cost. And to what end? To encourage him in idleness, to increase his insolence, to add fuel to the flame of race hatred, and to multiply his frightful records of crime against his would be, but misguided, benefactors.

Is book-learning then a mistaken policy and a curse to the feeble-minded Negro race? Unquestionably it is when carried to the ridiculous extremity of existing systems, and when regarded in the light of the absurd ends which it is intended to accomplish.

But there is a totally different side to this whole question of training the Negro away from manual labor, an aspect really pleasing to the most substantial element of Southern whites. It is true that this campaign of education, in alienating the Negro from his only source of substantial gain, and enticing him into the snare of the thriftless, roaming, idle life— thus rapidly increasing his mortality rate—is hastening the end of the problem by *augmenting* the *rate* of *relative* decline in *numerical strength*. Viewed in this light the otherwise nonsensical and burdensome policy may really be regarded as a blessing in disguise to all parties concerned.

The two great independent Negro schools (Hampton and Tuskegee) have been elsewhere briefly referred to; but constituting as they do the two principal foci of independent expenditure of the white man's substance, in an effort to elevate the Negro to the level of his superiors, a few general remarks may be advantageously added in connection with the subject of education.

Judging from casual observation and the testimony of several of its former students, it may well be doubted if the average student body of Hampton possesses as much as 50 per cent. of Negro blood. And we presume—for this is but a presumption —that the same statement holds good as regards its stalwart offspring—Tuskegee. The latter's moving spirit—Doctor Booker T. Washington—has certainly not more, and probably less, than 50 per cent. of Negro blood in his veins. We have recently discussed the question with a very intelligent and reliable colored man; in character, industry and ability decidedly above the average white man. This person is probably one-fourth Negro, one-fourth Amerind and the remaining half white man. He attended the Hampton school for three years and states that during that time he is quite certain that the average student was at least half white. Moreover he regards the pure Negro as far below the half-breed in intelligence, though the latter is generally more vicious and criminal, consequent, in part at least, upon a realization of his hopeless position as an inferior,—apart from individual worth—and especially because of his classification as a Negro. He also regards the mulatto as mentally and physically inferior to the pure-blooded white man, but holds that justice demands that they may be recognized as occupying an intermediate position between the two races.

In view of these facts Hampton Institute cannot be regarded as a fair test of Negro education and the use which he is capable of making of it; the conditions are entirely abnormal and artificial, and the student body is by no means uniformly Negroid.

Moreover the education of a few thousand Negroes and cross-breeds by such extraneous and artificial methods really has no special bearing upon the question when considered in connection with a race comprising ten million souls.

The very few so-called Negroes of distinction scarcely require mention in this connection.

In the first place few if any of them are really Negroes, and, secondly, these may almost be counted on the fingers of one hand. If there is any truth in the maxim that we must have a few exceptions in order to prove a rule we certainly came dangerously near being unable to produce the exceptions as a means of verifying our assertion regarding mental inferiority of the Negro race. We are not sure there has ever lived a pure Negro exceptionally distinguished for his intellectual powers. There are a very few men who have lived—and two or three men still living—of mixed blood who have attained such distinction.

In reviewing this list it has become sort of an arbitrary custom to begin with the name of the distinguished French novelist and dramatist, Alexandre Dumas, who happened to have a strain of Negro blood in his otherwise famous French ancestry.*

The distinguished novelist and dramatist may have had one-twelfth Negro blood, since it is probable his great-grandmother was a mongrel. But if it can be shown that this great-grandmother was a pure Negress the novelist was in all likelihood one-sixth part Negro. However, it makes no real differ-

---

*The Alexandre Dumas, whom we presume to be the one usually referred to as a Negro of distinction, was not a Negro at all.

His father, his paternal grandfather, and his paternal great-grandfather were all Frenchmen of exceptionally fertile brains, and all attained distinction. The great-grandfather was a wealthy Haitian colonist and it appears that he cohabited with a woman who is sometimes spoken of as a mulatto and sometimes as a Negress. Whether this relation was legitimate or illegitimate is a matter of dispute.

Now there seems to be the gravest doubt as to who is meant by Alexandre Dumas, as father and son were both men of great literary distinction having identically the same name. The father was a very great novelist and story teller, while the son achieved the highest honors as a novelist and dramatist.

This confusion seems to be due to ignorance on the part of those commonly referring to Alexandre Dumas as a distinguished Negro. When used for the purpose of glorifying the Negro race the reference should relate to the father who had very little Negro blood, but more of course than did the son.

ence whether he was one-sixth, or one-twelfth, or smaller percentage of African or Haitian extraction; enough has been shown to expose the absurdity of crediting the Negro race with his accomplishments.

Frederick Douglass is perhaps the next man reputed as a distinguished and able Negro. His father was a pure Anglo-American.

Paul Lawrence Dunbar was a poet of some note and it does not appear that any of his ancestors were white, but coming from a race of slaves it is quite impossible to prove that such was or was not the case.

Professor Dubois, of the Atlanta University, and William H. Lewis, recently appointed Assistant Attorney-General of the United States, are unquestionably men of exceptional ability; but what we have said in regard to Dunbar applies with equal force here, and while we have no information on the subject we feel sure that an investigation would reveal the fact that they are not pure-blooded Negroes. Lastly we have the name of Dr. Booker T. Washington, who says in his own writings that his father was a white man.*

Therefore it may correctly and justly be said that even under the most favored possible environs the Negro race has produced no great intellects.

There is no chance then for the Negro to rise to

---

*It has been contended by at least one writer on this subject that the disclosure of the fact that most so-called Negroes of distinction are of mixed blood, is not a valid argument against the capacity of the Negro to rise to a higher station in our national life; for the reason that the problem which we are facing has to do with mulattoes as well as pure Negroes. In this, however, the essayist is wrong, since not more than 15 per cent. of the Negro population can properly be regarded as mulattoes, which is something like 2 per cent. of our total population. And even this insignificant number, in addition to its tendency to return to the pure Negro stock, has been shown to be rapidly dying out.

the intellectual level of the white American; amalgamation is much further removed than it was at the close of our Civil War; deportation is almost impossible under all the circumstances.

We are able to discover no other solution than *racial decline* and ultimate *elimination* by *natural causes.*

CHAPTER XVIII

Proposed Solutions of the Negro Problem

EVER since emancipation there has been a luxuriant production of theories by which Southern white people might rid themselves of the burden thus imposed. We have sometimes wondered if it would now be possible to invent a plan for the extirpation or segregation of the American Negro, without infringing one or more of those already presented. Thus far the only good that has ever come of such inventions has been the added illustration of the fertility of the brains of our American people.

Among the suggested solutions most commonly before the public may be mentioned education (which usually means book-learning, rather than such manual and moral training as the Negro really needs), purposeful, or involuntary segregation, deportation and colonization, annihilation or violent extermination, John Temple Graves' theory of amputation, and more recently sterilization.

Most of those proffered plans of solution have been elaborately worked out by their authors, and some of them, when superficially considered, seem decidedly plausible; but very little reflection is needed to reveal the fact that not one is constitutional.

When theoretical details of the initiation of these suggested volitional solutions have been cast aside and the more serious aspects of the case are considered, we promptly emerge from the mists and fog which otherwise obscure their more vital relations.

Then mentally journeying into the poorly illumined future, but taking with us the candle of past events, our explorations can be made to reveal with clearness the fact that no plan has yet been presented, and that none is likely to arise, capable of metamorphizing into such proportions as to constitute a panacea for this most vital social and political disorder.

Present numerical strength, constitutional protection, and improved moral concepts of modern civilizations, serve to illustrate the remoteness of possible execution of proposed plans for colonization, either at home or abroad, against the will of the Negro race. Any one of the plans suggested for colonization could be carried out, even in opposition to Negro resistance, if all white citizens willed to do so, and foreign powers did not intervene. The physical barriers could be overcome. But the very conditions standing in the way of any attempt to execute these radical proposals form the crux of the whole situation.

Education is an insidious plan of solution having its birth in the fertile brains of some of our Northern brothers, and apparently intended to rise so high above the mental plane of Southern intellect as to completely escape the limitations of its supposedly restricted vision; but the mental atmosphere of the South is not now, and never has been, so hazy as to prevent a microscopic examination of its smallest details. Certain organizations of the North have been, and still are, actively engaged in sowing what they believe to be the seeds of destruction to our pure Anglo-Southern population. The label of these seeds is *education* and the fruit which they are intended to bear is *amalgamation;* but thus far they have all rotted in the barren soil of Negro character and the putrescent products of their decomposition have contributed much towards the physical decadence of that race. And if we may judge by the magnitude of these secondary products a persistence of such efforts will seriouslyyinterfere with the conclusions drawn from our investigations by the production of a geometrical ratio of racial decline to substitute our arithmetical basis of estimation.

Such education as the mass of our Negro population is now receiving is certainly a contributing factor in his ultimate extermination. Thus far education has had no perceptible tendency whatever to bring about the abomination of amalgamation, a result so confidently expected by certain educational societies having their origin in the North and the field of their nefarious operations in the South. As a matter of fact such illegitimate amalgamation as has taken place has never done more than produce a bastard mulatto race which is even more unfit than the pure Negro himself, and there has never arisen— even in the North—the slightest tendency to absorb this hybrid stock. Negro education, when general application is made, serves only in elimination by unfitting him for such occupations as are open to him and such as he is naturally suited to fill.

Involuntary segregation has never been attempted, and, in all probability, never will be. It is the most romantic and illogical expedient of all possible solutions yet advanced.

Such an attempt would be revolutionary, being in direct and open conflict with the Constitution. Moreover there exists no justifiable cause for this radical remedy. It is plain that the government could never set its seal of sanction to such a proposition, and revolt against the meanest of governments is always the last resort of a people oppressed beyond endurance. And certainly there can be none to propose that segregation be undertaken by Southern whites in opposition to the government, the North, and the ten million Negroes themselves. No good and enlightened citizen in any section of our common country would dream of advocating such a course, and a vast majority would resist the proposal with all the force of their being.

The only alternative then of effecting this, the most reasonable of all radical remedies, would be by alterations in the Constitution amounting almost to a rewriting of that instrument, an emergency for which the instrument itself provides. For various sections, amendments and clauses would have to be repealed and others totally different in fundamental principles substituted. Such drastic revisions would necessarily greatly abridge present guarantees of human rights wisely inculcated in that document, the probability of which are each and every one alike unreasonable and unthinkable.

Usually when a writer suggests colonization he apparently forgets the more serious aspects and difficulties involved, and elaborates on the costs and facilities for its physical performance. If we had to contend only with the physical obstacles standing in the way any plan could be executed, for we are a most powerful and resourceful nation.

Amputation (which of course means cutting off) has been proposed by Mr. John Temple Graves in a lecture delivered to a Chautauqua audience, and while we have never seen or heard this theory elaborated, it is safe to place it in the common category with other radical proposals, as not likely to be at any time seriously considered.

The theory of annihilation, or violent extermination, was a product of Reconstruction times, and if other solutions of that dreadful condition had not speedily presented, the outraged South might, ultimately, in its desperation, have ventured upon this perilous attempt. But all possibility of this reign of terror and bloodshed passed from the field of contemplated solutions many years ago. Even this could have been done at the sacrifice of many men and half the women and children of the land, if by any means the constitutional requirements of governmental intercession could have been held aloof, and the people of other states and foreign countries debarred from intervention, which latter are conditions too absurd to discuss. Duty would have necessitated the arrest of this wholesale murder by those who made the conditions provoking it.

This suggested solution then, if it ever had a serious aspect, is long since past and gone forever.

Sterilization of one or both sexes has been proposed by some extremists, and if the Negro race and the rest of the nation unanimously supported it nothing could be simpler or less costly. But apart from its unconstitutionality and the resistance which other sections would necessarily offer,—even if the South itself were ready and willing to attempt it— it would involve that section in a most hideous and sanguinary race war; a veritable death-grapple between the two races, and if uninterrupted would result in the more or less complete and violent extermination of the weaker and frightful losses to the stronger. The very suggestion of this racial sterilization is too unreasonable to require serious refutation.

Lastly it has been suggested to the writer—by a most capable man—that a plan of segregation could be formulated and carried out without disturbance of any kind. This plan proposes to establish the

Negro race in some part of our own territory, or in some contiguous territory acquired for the purpose, preferably some island, such as Cuba. Under this plan the expatriated race is to be made to realize that the scheme contemplates its benefaction quite as much as the relief of the white man of his objectionable presence. The Negro is to be securely established and made a self-governing community.

This plan contemplates the passage of a law by the National Congress to the effect that all Negroes born after a certain date be removed at maturity to a selected spot and there provided a small home by the government of the United States. The United States is to foster the new nation in every necessary way, including guarantees against both foreign interference and internal dissension and violence.

The general conception of this plan provides that the details be so completely and elaborately worked out that the Negroes would be willing and anxious to depart at the age mentioned to inherit a home and full privileges of citizenship. He would be made to understand that he would be taken, with all his chattels, to a land of plenty; where he could exercise and enjoy *in fact,* the social and political prerogatives which at present are his only *in theory*.

It is further suggested that if the requirement that all new-borns be transported at a given age be regarded as too rapid a change, that the law be made to provide that only a certain per cent. of each generation be thus deported; or, that they be given a certain amount of choice as to whether they go or stay, but making their legal and social condition so much better in this land of colonization that all influences would conspire, as it were, to bring about the change.

In this *promised land* the Negro would run his

own government—electing his own officers and representatives—as fast as consistent with orderly government.

This plan, or something similar, is by far the best and most reasonable yet advanced; but it does not offer a solution of our Negro problem. For, in the first place, it—like the rest—is unconstitutional in its very conception.

We could not require them to go, nor could Congress offer such attractions as would supposedly induce them to voluntarily leave their present homes to accept gratuitous grants and equipment in territory set apart for this purpose; each proposition being alike without the constitutional powers of Congress. To compel them would be to abrogate their constitutional rights, and to induce them with material rewards would not conform to the provision of equal rights to all, unless it could be shown, or construed, that the rest of the American people received an equivalent in the improved social and economic conditions at home. Even if these conditions could be overcome we could not consistently deny the Negro the right to return at will.

If these objections could all be surmounted and such a proffer seriously tendered, only a small percentage of Negroes would probably accept. And of this number it is quite certain that many would return after the novelty and emotional excitement had passed. The whole argument is worse than useless for the further reason that only a minority of the members of Congress represent districts having a Negro problem, and many of them are still strongly in favor of equal rights for the Negro while living in our midst. Therefore, there is not the remotest prospect of the passage of such a law, even if it could be shown that Congress is wholly free from constitutional barriers.

If any scheme of internal or external segregation or colonization is ever effected it must be planned and executed by private enterprise, and in accordance with existing provisions of the Constitution. Such an undertaking by private individuals, or associations of individuals, is extremely improbable; and if proposed and seriously undertaken would, undoubtedly, meet with opposition on the part of the Negro race. Therefore, and in view of the circumstance that equal rights and equal protection are guaranteed to the Negro, along with all others, when added to his decided disinclination to migrate, effectually shuts off private enterprise in this direction. And such an attempt, without the support and perpetual guidance of our American government, would be destined to ignominious failure.

The republic of Liberia, founded in 1822, on the Grain Coast of West Africa, is an excellent example of such a scheme. Its promotion, while not directly under the United States government, was certainly fostered and encouraged by a class who had the support of those high in authority at Washington. The promoters of this scheme organized themselves into the "National Colonization Society of America," and began by colonizing free Negroes—but with the deeper and commendable purpose of ultimately destroying the institution of slavery in the United States. Among its members were to be found such influential names as Bushrod Washington, Robert Finley, Charles Carroll, James Madison, Henry Clay, J. H. B. Latrobe, Bishop Hopkins, Rufus King, Dr. Channing, Benjamin Lundy, Garrit Smith, and James G. Burney. John Randolph, of Roanoke, was also interested in the project, and Thomas Jefferson had suggested this, or a similar plan, in the year 1811.

It appears that this plan might have met with greater success had it not been crippled (about 1831, only nine years after the founding of Liberia) by the alienation of some of its strongest supporters, through the extreme radicalism of William Lloyd Garrison.

During the twenty-five years (1822-1847), of the active efforts of these influential Americans, only a few thousand Negroes were induced to enter upon the perilous venture, though no doubt transportation from America to this new land of liberty was pictured to the ignorant and credulous Negroes by over zealous enthusiasts on Negro freedom, as a change of relations closely resembling translation from hell to heaven.

In 1847 the new republic was left to its own resources, and in spite of a certain amount of protection afforded by the United States has proven an utter failure. The old, old story over again, of the Negro failing to make good when disassociated with intellectual races.

And this is the fate that awaits further attempts of private colonization of the Negro. He is born a dependent, a hewer of wood and a drawer of water, and such he must ever remain.

It has been shown then that every plan devised by the whites intended to rid themselves of the presence of the Negro population, is wholly insufficient to perform the tasks imposed, and that nothing short of a combined determination on the part of the white population of the entire country, and a remodelling of the National Constitution, could reasonably be expected to meet successfully the exigencies of the undertaking. And such a combination of forces and circumstances will never come to pass.

The Constitution provides that whenever two-thirds of both Houses of Congress shall deem it necessary, amendments may be by them proposed, or, on the application of the legislatures of two-thirds of the several States, the Congress shall call a convention for proposing amendments, which, in either case shall be valid to all intents and purposes as part of the Constitution, when ratified by the legislatures of three-fourths of the several States, or by conventions in three-fourths thereof, as the one or the other mode of ratification may be proposed by the Congress.

From this it may readily be seen that it is no easy matter to amend the National Constitution. It can be done, but the proposition has to be supported by the people and by the politicians throughout the country. It requires either two-thirds of the members of both Houses of Congress or the request of the legislatures of two-thirds of all the states to call a convention where amendments may be proposed. When this has been accomplished such proposed amendments must merit and win the approval of the National Convention; and when the Convention has agreed to such changes and amendments the same are only then ready to go back to the people for their further deliberation, where they must secure the support of at least three-fourths of the legislatures of all the states, or conventions of three-fourths of all the states, called according to the provisions of law, for the express purpose of considering the advisability of ratifying the work of the National Congress.

Thus it may be seen that while it is not impossible that a constitutional amendment, or amendments, as would be required in this case, be adopted in response to a general demand of this people that some one of the plans mentioned, or some other plan of solving the Negro problem, be made legal; yet on the other hand such a complete revolution of public sentiment, as would manifestly be necessitated, is so improbable as to justify the conclusion that it will never come to pass.

There exists no pressing need or general demand for it, and not the slightest probability that there will later arise such a demand or necessity. Therefore we deduct from the facts here exhibited the conclusion that no revolutionary, or constitutional attempt, will ever be made to force a complete separation of the two races. That one and all of the theories advanced are impracticable and unnecessary, and that such idle talk is worse than useless, and should be discountenanced in public places as harmful alike to both races, by reason of its obvious tendency to excite mutual animosities and to add fuel to the flame of race prejudice. Such discussions and speculations can never be fruitful of beneficial results. Such idle talk is worse than a mere waste of words; and apart from such use as the exhibition of the fact that those proposing them have never gone deeply into the complex influences that hedge about the situation on every side, they are hurtful to the friendly relations between the races, which should be encouraged and fostered by good citizens in every proper manner.

No one possessed of an unbiased and discriminating knowledge of the deeper facts relating to the Negro problem, can consistently conclude that there is the least justification for hoping that any one of the multifarious proffered plans of solution—by direct and purposeful intervention—can ever fructify into accomplished fact.

"A little learning is a dangerous thing;
Drink deep or taste not the Pierian spring;
There shallow draughts intoxicate the brain,
And drinking largely sobers us again."

CHAPTER XIX

The Natural Solution of the Problem

CENTRED about the primary fact of mental inferiority of the Negro, natural forces are, apparently, busily at work, solving the American race problem; not by preparing the way for any sudden catastrophe, or breach of comity between the races, nor by developing any condition necessitating *sudden* and *drastic action* on the part of the white population; but by a gradual and orderly *elimination* of the Negro through certain sociological disadvantages and his own lack of natural fitness; with a concomitant appropriation to itself, on the part of the white race, of a progressively larger share of accumulated wealth and desirable branches of industry.

The various influences combining to effect this solution have been systematically presented in each succeeding chapter of this work. The whole question hinges on racial qualities,—which includes racial advantages—and we believe the proof of greater natural fitness and greater social, political and economical advantages of the white race is implicit in the context.

Some have contended that the Negro is destined to dominate the field of agricultural labor in the South—in the future, as in the past—but we have shown that he is being rapidly crowded out here as elsewhere.

Mr. Alfred Holt Stone, of Mississippi, (in his "Studies in the American Race Problem") has given reliable evidence in substantiation of the fact that in certain cotton districts of the South, Italian immigrants have supplanted the Negro, almost without a contention of the ground, on the part of the latter. He produces the figures in substantiation of his statement that these immigrants can accomplish a great deal more work from the start by virtue of such qualities as industry, forethought, and regularity. He also shows that they can live better on less money.

It is not, however, contended that the time is come, or is even close at hand, when the Southern Negro will no longer be able to find employment of some sort in this field. His elimination will come to, pass—so far as it is to take place—through a gradual re-adjustment. He is now being supplanted as an agricultural laborer, but his dull faculties are scarcely able to detect either the fact or the cause. Each decade will witness a larger proportionate number of white laborers in the South and the great body of Negroes will find it increasingly difficult to earn sufficient money to meet their necessities—an economic condition tending slowly, but surely, to marked reduction in relative numerical strength of the Negro. This will finally result in his elimination as a serious race problem, but not, we believe, in absolute extermination.

While the Negro does not migrate in great numbers from one country to another, he is a natural rover within certain narrow limits, and as he finds his old position in the South occupied by the white man he will immigrate in increasing numbers into other states, seeking profitable employment; there, in many cases, to sicken and die because, in the first place, of his constitutional unfitness for climatic changes, (especially from hot to colder climates), in the second place, because of his lack of means to properly provide against the dangers of his new conditions.

The immigrant and the Northern settler in the South are in active competition with the Negro in the field of manual labor of every kind; while the Southern white man is rapidly passing from under the influence of the silly ante-bellum sentiment, that agricultural labor is disgraceful. There are of course occupations more highly thought of, and more remunerative, but none more honorable and respectable than useful manual labor. A man best fitted for physical labor, but who persistently refuses to pursue it, and, instead, leads a life of idle poverty, is an undesirable citizen. He cannot command the respect and high regard which all entertain for the honest laborer. This the Southern people are fast coming to appreciate, and consequently entering more and more into active and successful competition with the unreliable Negro in this field.

By reason of his inability, or unwillingness, to successfully resist these new and adverse influences the Negro is fast losing ground and losing his former position of practical monopoly of Southern farm labor.

Another important cause of Negro racial decline is volitional segregation, which has gone on steadily and progressively from the time he became a freeman. As he comes to live more to himself there is observed a marked retrogression, with a decided increase in his death-rate; while the absence of close contact of the two races improves the hygienic condition of the whites, and materially lessens its mortality rate.

Both Baltimore, Maryland, and Richmond, Virginia, have their *Africa* (a community composed almost exclusively of Negroes), and a similar ten-

dency is observed in all cities having a Negro population—whether large or small. In addition to this
natural segregation the white man has been forcing
the Negro back, by systematic regulations, ever
since emancipation. Both of the above named cities
have very recently adopted what is known as *segre-
gating ordinances,* by which the *Negro* is *forbidden*
to move into *city districts having* a *majority* of *white
residents,* or districts exclusively inhabited by whites.
Other cities will later take similar action. By these
means we have a progressive segregation movement
supported and encouraged by the Negro himself on
the one hand and demanded and exacted by the
whites on the other.

It is important in connection with the marked tendency of the American Negro to segregate into distinctively Negro communities, to note the natural
tendency—under such conditions—of a race or variety to return to former customs and habits of life.
The *natural consequences* of *Negro segregation*
have been more fully brought out in earlier chapters,
but it may be further stated in connection with this
important phase of *natural solution of the Negro
problem,* that the Negro is known to be neglectful of
hygienic surroundings when disassociated with the
white man, and that under such conditions he shows
a strong tendency toward a resumption of his former rude habits of life. In exclusively Negro communities that race is largely bereft of the encourag-
ing example and uplifting precept afforded by closer
contact with the superior race.

Ethnologists and anthropologists are agreed that
under present conditions of life there is a marked
tendency toward a much closer approach to a common type of man, which implies a corresponding
elimination of the unfit varieties. The keen compe-

tition and excessive activities of modern life leave little place for the thriftless sluggish Negro type. This tendency serves to maintain a much higher death-rate for our Negro population and can have no other meaning than that the Negro is being crowded out by existing sociologic and economic conditions.

In this process of *natural selection* (in the broadest usage of that term) there are certain types among the highest race that are to be gradually eliminated as the unfit, but with the passing of this white element, a much greater part of the Negro race is doomed to certain elimination.   This elimination will be marked by a continual *lowering* of *relative Negro increase,* and *finally* by an *actual decrease* in numbers.

As we have repeatedly said the primary cause of this *natural solution of the Negro problem* is to be sought and found in the established fact of his *mental inferiority.*   Other causes which have been mentioned, as well as those contained in the remainder of this chapter are but natural sequences of this fundamental truth.

Canada is now complaining of the number of Negroes annually crossing her border from the United States; but if she knew better the deeper causes of this migration, and the stress of circumstances compelling that element of our population to exchange a favorable for a most unfavorable climate, and the natural consequences to the Negro race of such climatic changes, she would have no fears of a *serious future Negro problem.*

When the Negro crosses the Mason and Dixon line—as many are now doing—it is in desperate search of some locality where competition is less keen and where race prejudice no longer militates against his very existence; neither of which conditions is to be found on this American continent.

The pressure of these adverse circumstances will finally scatter a considerable portion of Southern Negro population to the four winds, and whether the individual elects to go or stay these natural causes of his elimination remain constant.

To those who are not too greatly prejudiced the position of the emancipated Negro is decidedly pathetic: Educated away from his only hope of salvation, crowded out by white competition and hounded by race prejudice, he is unable to maintain himself atyhome, and worse conditions await him abroad.

We do not contend that during the present generation, nor even during twenty generations, the Southern Negro is to entirely disappear, but we believe it has been proven that he is to be restricted in numerical strength at present, and later to decline in actual numbers, and, finally,—and within the present century—to be so reduced in relative numerical strength as no longer to constitute a *serious American problem.* No house is large enough for two families. No nation is large enough for two races.

In further substantiation of this position the following personal letters from Mr. Frederick L. Hoffman, chief statistician to the Prudential Insurance Company of America, are introduced without alteration or abridgment:

(FIRST HOFFMAN LETTER—DATED AUGUST 5, 1910)

"You will find all the information which you desire in my book on the Race Traits and Tendencies of the American Negro, a copy of which can be obtained on addressing Mr. T. N. Carver, Secretary,

American Economic Association, Harvard University, Cambridge, Mass. The book was published in 1896 and the data have not been brought down to date, but I hope to have time to go into the matter again after the results of the census of 1910 are available. It requires to be said, however, that the great sanitary advance of the country as a whole, and of large cities in particular, has been of benefit to the Negro race, and that there has been a fall in the death rate from all causes but not to the extent of the corresponding decline in the death rate of the white population. I am in a position to say, as the result of extensive correspondence with Southern physicians and thorough personal investigation, that the physical condition of the race, particularly in the rural districts as well as in the cities, has deteriorated during the last generation, and that both tuberculosis and syphilis are extremely common. It is also true that drug habits have taken an immense hold upon the colored population in the South, particularly the men employed along the Mississippi river and the lumber camps of the Gulf States. Another unfavorable element is the increasing tendency toward criminal abortion and a diminished birth rate as the result of deliberate means as well as of a possible increase in physiological sterility.

"Our Company has not for a number of years insured Negroes except in cases where we were compelled to do so in compliance with the law. About fifteen years ago, beginning with Massachusetts, a number of Northern States passed anti-discrimination laws, which prohibited companies from charging a higher rate to Negroes than to whites, irrespective of the fact of an excessive mortality. The Prudential has not since that time solicited risks among the colored population, but, of course, if such risks offer themselves voluntarily and can pass the required medical examination they are accepted, but such cases are very rare.

"Although I have been quoted to the effect that the Negro will ultimately disappear, I am not of the opinion that that is likely to be the case. I am rather of the opinion that the race will reach a stationary condition, very much as is the case with the Gypsies in Europe, and to a certain extent with our Indian population. The enormous influx of new immigrants, with a high birth rate, will alone be sufficient to provide a natural increment of the white population far in excess of the corresponding increment on the part of the colored. As the disparity in numbers increases the Negro will tend to become more and more a negligible factor except in particular sections where the race has gained a numerical and predominating position."

(SECOND HOFFMAN LETTER—DATED AUGUST 17, 1910)

"You may make use of my letter of August fifth as you desire. In addition, however, I may call your attention to the following comparative death rates of the white and colored population, according to the mortality statistics of the Census of 1908. The information is for practically all of the cities of the United States, excepting certain very large cities in the North. According to this tabulation, which appears on p. 26 of the report of the Census Office for 1908, the entire death rate was 16.6 per 1,000, and the colored death rate 26.2. For Mobile, Ala., the rate was 17.3 for the white and 25.6 for the colored. For Washington, D. C., 16.2 for the white and 26.1 for the colored. For Atlanta, Ga., 18.7 for the white and 24.8 for the colored. Louisville, Ky., 13.9 for the white and 25.3 for the colored. New Orleans, La., 19.0 for the white and 32.8 for the colored. Richmond, Va., 18.8 for the white and 30.0 for the colored.

"These rates are sufficient to sustain the conclusion that, practically without exception, the death rate of the colored population materially exceeds the corresponding death rate of the white population at the present time.

"I can also give you the rates for certain Northern cities for 1908, which are as follows: Chicago, Ill., white 13.8; colored 25.0. Boston, Mass., white 18.9; colored 26.0. St. Louis, Mo., white 13.7; colored 26.4. New York, white 16.6; colored 28.9. Philadelphia, white 16.7; colored 30.2.

"The actual differences in all cases are really much greater, on account of the fact that the age distribution of the colored population is more favorable to crude low death rate than the corresponding age distribution of the white population.

"At present there are no data for recent years which permit of an analysis of the mortality by divisional periods of life."

In these letters we not only have very recent figures showing the tendency of Negro racial decline, but also the opinion of a man who has made a life study of these questions; both of which are confirmatory of our conclusions which have been reached by a comprehensive study of the deeper causes lying back of statistical evidence.

The wide-spread doctrine that the condition of the Negro—at least morally and physically—must be made as good as that of the white man—for the protection of the latter, if for no other reason—is a singular combination of logic and sophistry. If the whites were to be as closely associated with the Negro as they are with members of their own race there would be no denying a very much greater necessity for efforts in this direction than are demanded by actual conditions. The morals of the whites would then be influenced, to some extent at least, by the immorality of the Negro; and the health of the former would then be directly and seriously jeopardized by the diseased condition of the latter. But, close contact of the two races is now, and always has been, the exceptional relation—not the usual—and where such close contact still exists the tendency is strongly towards separation.

In freedom the Negro has shown an increasing tendency to racial segregation, and the few who attempt closer contact are repelled, and forced back, by concerted private action and statutory regulation on the part of the whites. Therefore the statement that both moral and physical necessities of the whites imperatively demand that Negro hygienic conditions be made equal to those of the higher race is a very false view to take of this feature of the problem. Its desirability, from a certain standpoint, is admitted, but its urgent necessity is as positively denied. The dreadful scourges that afflict the Negro race are to some extent a source of infection to their white neighbors, but the latter so successfully guard against this danger as to maintain a mortality rate very nearly, if not quite as low as that of communities having no Negro population. As for Negro morality, or immorality (more correctly, non-morality), it has little, if any influence, on the moral standards of the white race. But this statement of fact should not be considered an argument in favor of a slackening vigilance of the whites, as regards the moral and physical condition of their Negro neighbors. Improved standards of Negro life in communities composed of both races, certainly contribute to the health of the white element.

If we accept the verdict of statisticians and all others who have given the subject their attention—including the government authorities themselves—to the effect that the published figures of the census report covering the decade, 1870-1880, are inaccurate and that the Negro population declined in relative numbers during that period, the percentage of Negro population has declined in every decade since the year 1810; or from the time of the passage of a law by Congress restricting the importation of African captives.

This we regard a most powerful argument in favor of a continuation of a similar decline during the remainder of the present century. When we remember that during the period mentioned above we have had fifty years of Negro slavery, and fifty years of freedom, and that the period covers all sorts of conditions—yet without a single interruption, or reversal, of this declining percentage—and that the percentage of Negroes has fallen (in round numbers) from 19 per cent. in 1810 to 11 per cent. in 1900 (a still smaller percentage will be shown for the census of 1910) we hold that it is highly probable that a similar rate of decline will continue throughout the present century.

If our reasoning proves to have been accurate, the year 2000 will witness a Negro population of less than 3 per cent., which will be too small—especially in view of the then prospect of a continuation of this decline—to give either the Nation, or the individual, the least concern regarding the race question of the future.

We are aware that some still contend that this

decline in relative numerical strength is speedily to terminate, and others yet, who go still further and invent theories by which the tables are to be turned, and a reverse process issue in; but in view of the mass of verifiable evidence herein contained to the contrary we are unable to take them seriously.

If, then, our predictions be true, or even approximately true, it cannot be denied that we have pointed the substantial end of the Negro problem in the United States, and that, too, within the present century.

Let us review the points made in this chapter alone in support of *the natural solution of the problem*.

Established mental inferiority is given as the basis of the argument and the source of all minor influences tending to reduce the relative numerical strength of the Negro race.

The whites are shown to be better fitted in every way for the various occupations offering a means of earning a comfortable existence. This fact combined with the further fact that there exists a strong mutual race prejudice, prevents the Negro from having an equal chance with the white man. This combination of facts is causing the Negro to scatter into the North and West where conditions are even worse than in the South.

At the same time there is observed a mutual segregation in the country districts, and in the cities. Each race showing a tendency to separate itself from the other. This is illustrated by the Richmond "Africa" and a similar district in Baltimore. Then there is also shown a determined purpose on the part of the whites to force back that smaller element of Negro population who would intrude upon white residential sections. This is illustrated by the very recent invention of *segregation laws*.

The well-established tendency of modern life to cause a closer approach to a common type of Man —which means elimination of the unfit—is decidedly an adverse influence to the survival, or increase, of our Negro population.

Another evidence of a slackening rate of Negro increase, under the pressure of white competition and race prejudice, is the recent complaint of Canada of the large numbers annually crossing her border from the United States.

It is not here contended that the Negro race in America will speedily disappear, but rather that existing adverse influences will cause a continuation of his declining relative numbers. This position is strongly supported by the Hoffman letters introduced. (The Aino race of Japan is the best of evidence that a race can indefinitely endure—in reduced numbers—even in the face of a strong race prejudice).

Selfish motives do not demand that the white race strive to bring Negro hygiene and Negro morality up to the high standards of the former, as some have attempted to make it appear. Negro immorality has little or no bearing on the white man's ethical standards. His physical uncleanliness certainly has some influence on the health of his white neighbors, but it is shown that this is slight under the rigid vigilance of the latter to protect itself against this danger.

On the other hand—and apart from the moral question involved—a great many white people in localities having a large Negro population look upon each individual Negro as a source of constant menace to themselves, and therefore have not the slightest objection to the prevalence of pestilence, diseases and death among that race, so long as they (the whites) feel reasonably safe from contamination.

The white race is not, as a rule, in sufficiently close contact with the Negro for diseases to spread rapidly from the one race to the other; and the bonds of union and association are being continually lessened and severed.

CHAPTER XX

Summary and Conclusion

IN THE early chapters of this work we have given the reader an outline of the important facts concerning the origin of the human species and the nature of its early development. The object of this is to show on the one hand that the Negro type has from the very beginning been the most backward division of the race; and on the other, that the Caucasic type has come to its position of superior intelligence and physical fitness for all climates, by untold ages of slight natural adaptational changes to vastly more varied conditions. This feature of the subject is regarded as one of the fundamental elements concerned in the solution of the Negro problem by natural causes.

After showing that until very recently—and to a great extent even now—the geographic domain of the Negro has been tropical, or semi-tropical, and therefore adverse to mental advancement, we have taken up the subject of the African stock from which our American Negro was chiefly drawn. This stock is shown to be incapable of producing a civilization of any kind. Unassociated with the white man it is believed by some to exhibit a tendency toward greater depths of degradation.

Then it is also shown that the methods employed in the capture of these Negroes tended to supply the African trader with the very lowest stratum of this barbarian race for transportation as chattels to the American colonists—a class largely held as slaves by the savages themselves.

The horrors of the "middle passage," and early colonial treatment of slaves, are shown to coincide with the rest of his history as tending to *prevent*, rather than to *cause*, mental or moral improvement of any kind.

Harsh laws for the early regulation of slavery in America are also shown to have been a further adverse influence.

Following out this line of investigation we have presented in the fourth and fifth chapters a scientific investigation of the Negro brain and of Negro mental faculties, and the facts thus revealed are found to be in perfect harmony with the previous history of that race. His brain is found to be decidedly smaller than that of higher races. The anterior lobes— the thinking part—are even disproportionately smaller; so much so that his skull is described as egg shaped, with the pointed end forward. Moreover the eight bones that collectively form the osseous covering of the brain become united in the Negro about the twelfth year, encasing the brain in a rigid wall and making its further development impossible; while in the higher races these bones remain more or less separate up to the fortieth year, permitting a continuous development until the meridian of life is past.

Many other scientific facts are given as concrete proof of the self-evident fact of mental inferiority of the Negro type.

Still further on it is shown that the makers of the National Constitution were well aware of the iniquity and folly of the institution of unlimited slavery, and while evading the whole question, so far as possible, only recognized human chattelism as the lesser of evils in a choice between an attempt to repudiate slavery and a failure to inaugurate the Constitution. In fact any other course would have meant defeat for both the ratification of the Constitution and the effort to abolish the institution of slavery. The South was ready to repudiate the proposed Constitution if its provisions interfered in any way with the holding of slaves.

Lincoln expressly recognized Negro inferiority, but fought for justice and the guarantee of natural rights to all men, as outlined in the Declaration of Independence and in the Constitution.

The circumstance that the Negro race took no voluntary part in the struggle for his freedom, even after the issue of Lincoln's *Emancipation Proclamation,* is further evidence of *racial inanition.*

The sequences of the Civil War threw the Negro in open and active competition with the white man for gain, and had it not been for a certain spirit of generosity on the part of the latter, a very great part of the Negro population would have promptly perished.

Thus it is seen that *Emancipation* and *Reconstruction* set in motion the forces that served to maintain a high Negro mortality rate, which forces, in the end, will suffice to solve the vexatious problem with which this work is concerned.

The purpose to tell what we conceive to be the whole truth fearlessly, and without regard to sectional feeling or individual differences is made plain.

The process of gradual crowding out by which the *Negro* is *being eliminated* is shown to be in complete harmony with the natural law of the *survival of the fittest.*

Continuing the pursuit of a connected argument it is shown that in every separate decade for a hundred years past the relative numerical strength of the Negro in the United States has declined; and that a continuation of a similar rate of decline will relieve this nation of a serious race problem before the end of the present century.

The accuracy of all these deductions is still further supported by impartial statistics presented, and by the Hoffman letters introduced.

After showing that at least seventy-five per cent. of all the people must, in obedience to an inexorable decree of nature, continue to occupy themselves with the performance of manual labor we conclude that the master race—having much too large an educated class of its own—will in future, as in the past, retain to itself practically all positions calling for the useful application of book-learning.

It is likewise further concluded that since the Negro race is poor it must—if it would survive and prosper, even in reduced numbers—apply itself to the earning of its daily bread, and there being no opportunity to do this, other than by manual labor, education, above the three Rs and away from the work that its highest interests demand that it assiduously pursue, necessarily militates against the survival of the race.

In support of the whole argument the fact is brought out that few, if any, Negroes have ever become exceptionally distinguished.

The more conspicuous among the various plans of solution of the problem, by direct white intervention, are taken up and each in turn refuted as too improbable to be regarded seriously.

The work of the National Colonization Society of America in establishing the Negro republic of Liberia, in Africa, is reviewed as additional evidence of Negro inferiority.

Mental inferiority is again declared to be the

great central truth in the many contributing causes to the natural solution of the problem.

Close contact of the two races is shown to be constantly lessening as a result of the respective segregation of each to itself. This segregation is both voluntary and enforced, thus constituting an ever increasing cause of Negro retrogression.

The causes of natural elimination of the Negro presented in this work apply in great measure to the South African race problem. There are certain elements, such as climatic fitness and a preponderance of Negro population (amounting to 8 to 1 in favor of the Negro) in South Africa, which serve to make that problem slower, but it seems to be only a matter of a greater length of time when the whites will there also greatly exceed the blacks in numerical strength.

Summing up then, and contemplating as a whole, that which the successive chapters have presented in parts we are able to see how each minor group of truths falls into its natural place within some major group, and how all major groups fit into their several places about the grand central fact of *mental inferiority* of the *Negro race*.

Finally then, and in conclusion, we believe the following facts have been abundantly demonstrated: That the Negro is very decidedly inferior to the white man in mental capacity; that there is a decided tendency towards a more or less complete elimination of the American Negro as an unfit element of our population; and that the causes operating to bring about this solution of the *Negro problem* will persist, and, ultimately—and within the present century—so reduce the relative numerical strength of that race as to have removed the Negro problem from the field of serious national questions.

Whether or not we have taken into account all the influences concerned in this sociological problem and given each its proper valuation, remain for the impartial and discriminating reader to definitely determine.

www.ingramcontent.com/pod-product-compliance
Lightning Source LLC
Chambersburg PA
CBHW050804270326
41926CB00025B/4530